I WAS A SPY

I WAS A SPY

by

MARION MILLER

THE **BOBBS-MERRILL** COMPANY, INC.
A SUBSIDIARY OF HOWARD W. SAMS & CO., INC.
Publishers • INDIANAPOLIS • NEW YORK

To my children and their generation

Acknowledgments

THIS book is part of a life. Many persons helped make that life more bearable. To name some would lead to the inadvertent omission of others, and this last I do not care to risk. Especially I do not want to risk endangering those who cannot be named by me now or ever. But my obligation to all is enormous—and they all know it.

I appreciate more than I can say the friendship of the Los Angeles press, both metropolitan and neighborhood newspapers.

I can never forget the unwavering faith of my mother, Ida Sweetwine Freed, who never asked the questions she must have wanted to.

To the men of the Los Angeles office of the Federal Bureau of Investigation go my sincere thanks for their inspiration.

In the preparation of this book, I am grateful for the editorial assistance of John Maynard.

MARION MILLER

Los Angeles

CONTENTS

PART ONE

"This Is Your Life"

WHEN I WAS THIRTY-SIX YEARS OLD I RAN AWAY from home. That's quite a bit beyond the normal running-away-from-home age but my need for escape was as fierce as it had been when, at four, I trudged out of Miami with seven cents and a doll for company. My parents brought me back that time. My husband, Paul, with a certain amount of collaboration from TV star Ralph Edwards, did the job now. My parents had the easier time.

Of course, this time was nowhere near as decisive in my mind, though somewhat more complicated. In Miami I positively was abandoning forever the cruel world of my childhood for some imagined oversight, and it was all of an hour and a half before they caught me. Now I was abandoning no one and, on that bright day in early spring, nothing. For everything surely had abandoned me. Already I had said goodbye to hope, and the flight really was a flight to nowhere, like so many. But in the conventional ways I was burning no bridges nor leaving loved ones behind me. We left on a Tuesday—Paul was with me—and would be back Thursday. We were going simply and specifically to Laguna Beach, California, ninety minutes by car, and by car is how we went. My children, Paul, Jr., Betsy and Bobby, were properly in the care of my mother.

But in another sense it was all a dreadfully final thing. There was nothing behind, so far as I could see, and just as certainly nothing ahead. Paul is a happy man and made happy talk about a second honeymoon, but I could not oblige him even by smiling. My world had turned on me and it was no use to say that I had suffered its hatred because I loved it. Others may have bigger worlds; mine, outside my home, is my friends and neighbors. To them I had said in my own way, I love you. To a few I said even that I love my country, which is a pretty schmaltzy thing to say when you come to think of it. A handful believed this, a small handful understood. The rest hung up.

Hatred, suspicion, distrust—these can fester anywhere. Yet where I lived then, and still live, they would seem miscast. But why? The womb of misgiving needs no special kind of climate. Our home is on Esther Avenue in West Los Angeles—what is called the Rancho Park section. It is a clean and pleasant street, curved gently by the subdividers to give it a touch of the bucolic. The houses are neat and architecturally individual, in the twenty-thousand-dollar class, forty-foot fronts, garages, nice little backyards that you get to call gardens if you've lived in L.A. a while. When the trees the city has planted grow, we will be a little pastoral. You do not look or listen for the evil whispers of disbelief or the shouted curse of anger, let alone the dark currents and tiny tributaries of conspiracy.

No, it's a street of lawn-sprinklers, the mailman's stop, the thud of the morning paper. It is, if you lead the right life anyway. Maybe that's where I got mixed up. Many well-adjusted people today are not sure I have led the right life. They consider it an error not of right or wrong but of judgment. They do not say I should have stayed under the bed and kept my mouth shut, but that is what they mean.

It is no more than fair to them, in fact, to look at Marion Miller, Laguna-bound, on the morning of March 24, 1956. For the better part of five years it has been a matter of "common knowledge" among certain ones that Marion Miller is a Communist. Until mid-October of the autumn before it has been a matter of established fact within the Communist Party of the United States. Agents of the Federal Bureau of Investigation knew better but these had superb reasons for not talking.

Now at last the Communists knew better, too, and a bullet to kill had been fired into the family room of my house when, for a wonder, no one was in there. A neat package of indescribable filth had been left on my doorstep. Letters had been received—and are still received nearly every day—full of vituperation and obscenity, now and then handsomely written, constructed of artfully balanced venom. Anonymous, of course, although often we know who the writers are. They're not kidding, those writers, they are not merely cranks. Those who say they wish me in hell do wish me in hell. The jolly postman doesn't look so jolly as he once did; not to me. There are phone calls in the morning and the afternoon, and just before dawn: Marion Miller, you're going to hate the day you were born; yes, and that fink husband of yours, and the day your children were born. Think of what I say, Mrs. Miller, tale-spiller, think of it tomorrow when your children are in school. Think of it every time your children are where you can't see them.

These are the judo blows of terrorism, like something in a B movie except they do not sound so much like silly melodrama to one whose life since 1950 *has* been something like a B movie. In time, nothing the phone can do can surprise you. But when, as I did—and Paul did—you join the Communist Party for the purpose of working undercover for the FBI, there is attrition of another sort as well. At least there was with me. It is the attrition of being isolated.

Paul and I are sociable people and like most sociable people, we have a sizable quota of friends. As the years after 1950 went on and I submerged deeper into the ooze of the Communist ditches, these fell away. By no means all of this was due to ostracism. Indeed that spread rather slowly in proportion to the rumor. But I found out very early in the game—this game that was not a game—that Communists are inveterate holders of meetings. They will meet for any reason or none, in groups of from two to two hundred. (The average "cell," or club, is about eight.) To each of these meetings I was summoned curtly by my master, the Party, whose beckoning finger is law. Some weeks there were four and five compulsory nights out. When I got home—the meetings rarely broke up before midnight and in Los Angeles everything seems to be half an hour from everything else—there was the business of typing out my report for the FBI while my findings were fresh in my mind. How under these strictures could we entertain or accept invitations?

So, much of the time, movement and exhaustion precluded loneliness and self-pity. But there would come weeks when my "friends" in the movement would let up for a while and we would have evenings at home. Evenings free, even, if anyone should ask us out. But no one did. Slowly that became the shocker. Paul and I had never got or expected loving cups for popularity, but our social life has been a full one. Now it was a nothing one. We sat, night after night, he and I and the children, and the children went to bed early. Persons who used to call us didn't any more, and when in something like desperation I called them, I sensed their withdrawal, their wish to say goodbye. In fright I began pressing, as the golfers say. My manner on the phone became nervously eager and then sycophantic, until Paul put a stop to that by telling me in so many words never to crawl to anyone again, for any reason. I could not say what was true without betraying myself—not to mention others: that I was not a Communist but an agent for the FBI and hence my country. I could not, in fact, do much of anything but what I was doing. I will tell about it all later as our story goes forward, but in this chapter alone I just want you to get the picture. As our enforced desolation became clear to me, my nervous system slipped its first cog. I turned to Paul one night, intending to say something with anyway a bit of tone, like, "Oh, honey, I can't go on!" Instead I said, "What have you got me into?"

A fine heroine I turned out to be. But that was nerves talking. Paul hadn't done it. The acquiescence had all been mine. Paul had condoned my decision, yes, and there will always be a question in both our minds whether or not I would have gone ahead if Paul had not been a counter-agent for many years before me —that comes later, too. But if I had not wanted to do what I did, I wouldn't have.

From that point on, my physical health deteriorated. I slept badly when I had time to sleep at all, and did considerable screaming while I was at it. Waking I was edgy as a cat at a kennel show. I lived each day closer to the edge of peril, not merely my own but my loved ones' as well, should discovery come at a critical time. I lost weight along with appetite until it appeared that if I shed one more pound I would simply vanish. I was saved from this in the spring of 1955 by collapsing with duodenal ulcers and related disorders. When after a month I left the hospital, it was agreed by all that my career as a poor man's Mata Hari was over.

It wasn't—quite.

It is true there are difficulties in extricating oneself from the

Communist Party but my way, so far as this one break was concerned, was made easy. The Government asked me to testify publicly for a case it was preparing—in brief, to blow the whistle on my former associates where anyone interested could hear the blast. I think I can say that the Communists were interested.

I did my stuff in Washington in early October of 1955. Except for the Communists, my testimony was met at first with a wave of indifference. From the objective point of view, it was not newsworthy. I knew of no pumpkin papers and could not say out of knowledge or belief that Moscow had infiltrated the Cabinet. There can be and there is such a thing as workaday espionage, however dramatic and dangerous it may be to the person involved, and mine was that. The press coverage of my pedestrian revelations was neglible.

Frankly, I hoped for a little better—and in time I was going to get it—but for a reason not connected with the aggrandizement of Marion Miller. I wanted it known to my friends at last that I was not what they had suspected, that the contrary was true, and there is nothing so resolutely convincing as one's own newspaper.

My position can best be put very simply, though I am sticking my neck out if it is read carelessly. "Everyone" had thought I was with the Bad Guys. Now they would know I'd been with the Good Guys all along, indeed working against the Bad Guys. That knowledge, once disclosed, would change everything. Easy as A-B-C. Those who had distrusted me would come to make amends with tears in their eyes. Strong men would crumple in shame. Loving hands would bedeck me in American flags. None of this was what I had sought nor what I do seek, but so long as the truth was going to be made known, I could see no harm in its being known in a loud voice.

It was, eventually. But my fantasies were for a long time just that, even afterward. The world, my world, did not beat a path to my door. The ostracism and distrust continued on the one side and the virulent hatred mustered and directed by the Communists gained momentum on the other. The last I had expected but the first was incredible and deeply shocking. My naïveté in conceiving that this was and is a matter of Good Guys and Bad Guys has not been shaken yet. I believe it with classic simplicity. If I am wrong, if I have been working for the wrong side, then this is a grave misfortune for me and a tragedy for civilization. But I am not wrong.

Nevertheless, the one quarter that did not shrug aside my Washington testimony was the Communist press. On the day I flew back to Los Angeles, the *People's World*, the Communist paper in Los Angeles, devoted half a column in bold-face type to what I had done. Their account of "betrayal" was not constrained. It was written with some of the disciplined objectivity of a heat-crazed elephant. But it was nothing beside a mimeographed attack distributed a few days later by the specific group on whose members and activities I had been gathering information. This sheet of paper, what promotion men call a flyer, reached hundreds of my friends and former associates by mail or door-to-door methods. In sum, it averred that I was the dregs of humanity. I will present it here verbatim a little further on. In the direct epithet category it called me a spy and an informer.

These, to revert to my favorite simplicity, were intended as "bad" words. All right, let them be. I have no patience with the sophistry of semantics. I *was* a spy. I *was* an informer. There are spies and informers in any war, and this surely is a war. I am content to let it rest there. The accusation that I was a thief is something else again. Oh, I never was technically guilty of burglary. But I did copy and disseminate privileged documents. The handbooks say mustn't.

Many "thieves" are jailed as a consequence of their actions. I became by and by, I am told, the most decorated woman in America. I say this not in irony but to point out that if one side can throw away the book, so can the other. This country is not so constricted by an inflexible moral code as its enemies would like to think. We are not above fighting fire with fire, as the incident of the American flier over the Soviet just before the Summit debacle last May so plainly showed.

I must say just the same that the Communist offensive against me was terrifyingly effective for many weeks. The ostracism by the Good Guys gave way to attack (the Communists, of course, exploded in naked ferocity). Even my friends, those who never had doubted, having heard no rebuttal to the Reds' "open letter," had no recourse but to wonder. The old doubters doubted even more.

This goaded Paul finally into an explosion of his own. The FBI —we call it The Bureau—quite naturally likes its operatives to keep quiet, whatever duress may press upon them. You cannot blame it for this. But perhaps you can't blame us for not being heroes either. I'd had it up to here with heroism. Paul, suffering even worse because a loved one was affected rather than himself, did what he had to do.

Paul, besides being engulfed in righteous anger, has a talent for public relations and decided to use it. He engaged the sympathies of some neighborhood papers, and these carried my true story in detail. He then went to the major Los Angeles dailies. For the most part they were just as sympathetic. Within a week I was a celebrity of sorts. It is an oddly exhilarating feeling, with a side effect of being divorced from oneself. The mail didn't fit in the mailbox, the phone now poured forth praise as well as invective—Communists have strange energies, so still the invective ran ahead about four-to-one—and the unknown person fired at us with the unknown rifle. We and our children came under police and FBI vigilance, and have been under it from that day forward.

But now, I thought, with all the terror, all the vileness, now will come the about face. Any day now, any hour, any week, committees will come bearing wreaths. Can they hold out forever? The sound of the phone will shift from a menacing jangle to a happy summons, and voices will say, "We're having friends over Wednesday and we were wondering if . . ." Now at the very least someone will say, "Thank you, Marion."

And someone did. A small number. But they were drowned out by the snarls of spy and Cossack, liar and thief, Gestapo lackey, and that cute little nosegay, Fascist bitch.

But these were the voices of the enemy, the avowed enemy. What of the friends, whose way of life was mine and which seemed to me so infinitely precious? Where were they? As I say, a few came filing back. And strangers, wonderful strangers who had divined a little of what I had done, called or wrote and lifted our hearts. But so many——Oh, why? Why?

Well, even a hysterical question deserves some kind of answer.

There were those who still were impressed first and foremost by the Communist flyer, that paean of vengeful scorn and hate. The grim thunder of sneak and thief and stool-pigeon still held them. They were convinced, as they were supposed to be convinced, that I had sold out a foreign-born minority. We'll get to all that. We'll get to everything.

There were those who thought that all the clubs I had ever belonged to I had joined for the purpose of spying for unnamed political police and smearing innocent persons—a retroactive indictment.

There were those who thought I had brought disgrace, or at best an undesirable and raffish kind of publicity, to the Jewish faith, which is my faith, Paul's faith.

There were those, I think, who were only shamed into turning away by having believed of me what they did.

There were even those, and for them I have pity, who were jealous—jealous of the headlines they wrapped the next day's fish in.

But then I did not understand.

And so it went all that fall and into the spring of 1956, when the crying spells began. I would cry and cry and feel no better for it. Some of the children were giving Paul, Jr., a bad time in school. Little Betsy was puzzled. Bobby was a baby; he alone didn't care.

That Halloween, I remember, there was a children's bazaar in the school yard. Each mother had a table to sell knicknacks for an unquestionably worthy cause. My table became a desert, a little spot of nothing in the middle of all the bustle. So determinedly was I avoided that the experience became a conspicuous agony, much worse because Paul, Jr., and Betsy were on hand to witness it. What could I tell them? What could I tell young Paul when he asked that night, "Mother, are you really a spy?" Yes, dear, but not the way you mean. You'll understand it all some day. Go to sleep now.

Esther Avenue was as serene as ever. The sun rose bright, the sky was blue. The sprinklers whirred, and the man across the street still turned his back and walked into the house if we passed by—but serenely. The hate mail tapered off a little but still stuffed the mailbox; the Communists are tireless. The menacing phone rang twenty times a day at the same ratio: four against, one for, a smattering of wrong numbers. The Bureau was kind and noncommittal. The papers had long since turned to something else. But not us. Paul and I and the Communists—we were still on the merry-go-round.

If there is any basic feeling of desolation, holidays sharpen it. T. S. Eliot said April is the cruelest month. I will always think December. Christmas of 1955 we got by. We ate and breathed and lived and had the children with us. Nothing's ever a total loss, I guess, unless all hope should go. But, oh how I hated that Christmas!

Then right after the holiday season, I think in early January, Paul began not being Paul. He was furtive and tense. He ended phone conversations if I walked into the room and went on errands he could barely account for. If it had not been Paul, I might have suspected an affair. But Paul is of me as I am of him. He is a handsome and charming man but never unfaithful. If I had ever thought it, it would have been then, and out of despair and the self-pity that at last had caught up with me. But I did not think it. If I thought anything, it was that Paul had snapped under the strain and had begun stalking gremlins.

One day, I remember, he sent me over to my mother's on a bit of business that made no sense whatever. Another, a man and woman called purporting to represent a well-known magazine and spent two hours interviewing me. Their questions were searching and sensible but they didn't seem to know the name of their editor. Later I was able to link up all these casual oddities, but not then.

It was in the third week of March that Paul suggested we get away together, just he and I, if only for a few days. It was more than a welcome suggestion; it came at a time when I was ready to climb the walls if I couldn't get outside them. We made reservations at the Surf and Sands Hotel in Laguna Beach for Monday through Thursday, the 27th, and arranged that the children be looked after. I wasn't happy about leaving the children, but if this was going to be a therapeutic measure, it was going to be one in every way. We got off in about the style you would expect—Paul forgot half his luggage and I half mine—and drove slowly down the coast.

Part of that drive, the last part after you've cleared the oil wells south of Long Beach, is beautiful, and for a while I was caught in a suspension of time, the way you are on a long train trip where for the hours between departure and arrival strain and responsibility are abdicated. There is nothing you can do about what is behind or what is ahead. It was one of the rare intervals in that time in which I told myself not to worry *and didn't.*

We drove slowly past Newport Beach and Balboa, on down U.S. 101, up the lovely climbing curve of Emerald Bay and into Laguna. Suddenly I could smile again. At the hotel we rested and sunbathed and ate too much and slept till we awoke. Home knew where to get us. No one else did—or so I thought.

But on Wednesday morning about ten Paul got a phone call. It was from a Mr. Don Malmberg, I learned later, who evidently had been persuasive enough to learn where we were. Paul talked for two or three minutes, hung up, and said Mr. Malmberg, "of Cleveland," had an offer for Paul of fifteen hundred dollars worth of business. Paul is a poster artist and, if I may be permitted a plug, a good one.

In the drowsy unreality of sea and surf, I bridled. "Can't it wait? We're supposed to stay through tomorrow!"

"Fifteen hundred dollars means nothing?"

Fifteen hundred dollars meant something. And I was beginning to chafe about the children. We packed, I without much zest, and made a strange trip home. The drive down had been rocket-like next to it. Paul dawdled and fussed. We stopped to watch a blimp land. We stopped at two drive-ins. He even stopped to get his hair cut!

"Are you sure," I asked finally, "fifteen hundred dollars means something? Why didn't we go by way of Tijuana if we have this much time?"

"I told you," he said, "we don't meet Malmberg till six-thirty. That restaurant at Sawtelle and National."

"Then why start so early?"

"Because," he said. "Now be a good girl and enjoy the scenery."

To this day Paul alone knows all the ramifications of that trip and the weeks before. I was conscious dimly only of delay and very dimly that certain cars, always in pairs, seemed to join and flank us at various stages, never dropping ahead or behind much. I didn't know that our lives had been threatened, should we complete the journey home. Paul did, but he couldn't stop now. Only next day was I to learn from the papers we had been under police surveillance every minute and so was my home and what was there. The Communists had learned of the event that I of all people must not hear of.

We met Mr. Malmberg at the appointed restaurant at six-thirty sharp. I gave him the look that women save for spoilers of second honeymoons but he smiled away the strain in the atmosphere. He must catch a plane, he said, so Paul would please make his pitch as fast as he could. Paul told him of the signs he would do and how he would do them and when delivery could be expected. Then, as both looked at their watches, Paul said, "But the colors you'll have to see for yourself. No one can explain colors. Follow us home, it's only a few blocks from here. My garage is my studio." *Colors*, I learned afterward, was the key word.

We turned off National, Malmberg following, north on to Westwood Boulevard, then east again on to Esther. Looking back as we turned, I thought that Malmberg's lights had vanished. Then I faced ahead and could see nothing but my house. Nothing.

It lay two hundred yards or so ahead, on our right. For a minute it didn't get home to me that it was ours. Then I knew that it was, with an appalling certainty that was worse than doubt. There were crowds and high, hard lights, police cars and what appeared to be a terrible confusion. There was the air of catastrophe, accomplished or imminent.

I screamed, and thought first, our house is on fire! Paul's face over the wheel had gone white and strained. Queerly, to my mind, he looked at the clock on the dashboard. It was one minute to seven. Headlights came toward us in a rush and Paul swore and pulled aside; Esther Avenue is not wide. The oncoming car brushed our fender and sped past, building speed. Instantly there was the growl-into-whine of a police siren, and quick pursuit.

"Who was it?" Paul said. "Did you get a look at that car? Who was it?" Who could tell? It was dark.

"I don't know, I don't know!" I'd never been so scared. "Paul, they've bombed our house! I know it! One of them's bombed us! Oh, my God, hurry!"

"No," he said. He was quiet again. "No one has. Now if you ever took it easy, take it easy for the next minute." He pulled to the curb and reached over to push open the door on my side, but I was way ahead of him. I jumped out. The movies of that arrival are a prized possession of mine. My face was contorted. I was a screaming, terrified woman, not more, not less. For the benefit of any Congressional committees I may face in the future, I say now that *that* was not rigged.

"My children! The children! What's happened?"

Very, very vaguely I was aware of professional lighting, a television set-up, a famous face bending solicitously over mine. I don't imagine that particular famous face had ever been quite so decomposed in public view—and it was so. He'd been nervous about that moment.

"My name is Ralph Edwards," said the famous face uncertainly in the famous voice. "If that helps any?"

I saw then that he was. I think I even knew, with a little wisp of realization, what it was all going to be about. Maybe not. But he saw me get back a measure of my aplomb and promptly got back all of his.

"Marion Miller," he said, "this is your life!" And we turned and walked into the house together—March 28, 1956, 7:00 P.M. exactly, Pacific Standard Time.

Ralph Edwards: that was a *high point* of my life, and thank you so much for it. But *this* is my life—the pages that lie ahead.

2

A Groundwork for Betrayal

IF YOU DO WHAT I DID, CONSPIRE ACTIVELY AGAINST the Communist Party, you are going to be asked sooner or later: Why? It's a reasonable question. There is nothing suspect about decrying the Communist Party and to decry it by means of a forum, should one happen to have a forum, is usually considered praiseworthy, the act of an aggressively normal American. But to take the field against it on its own conspiratorial terms, eschewing forensics and public expression of moral outrage and alarm—this needs explaining. There is something sinister about it. Those who have questioned me as to motive have never been rude enough to suggest that they know the addresses of one or two sound psychoanalysts, but there has been a tendency to send the children away as soon as they've said hello to Aunt Marion.

It would be convenient for me to say here that something in my youth or childhood made of me what is called a premature anti-Communist; but nothing did. Indeed I very definitely was not a premature anti-Communist. If I were to attach any label to my intellectual development, it would be that woefully ill-defined term "liberal." In my case I mean to say only that I was quite successful at seeing both sides of a given question. The anti-anti-Communists of today have the same form of debilitation. It made me rather ineffectual and perhaps even nondescript but obviously it had nothing to do with militant anti-socialism. I was even a little hurt when I came to learn that Communists despise liberals. It sounded treacherous and ungrateful of them. The liberals I have known are tolerant of anything as long as it is not intolerance. I felt that way too until I became an intolerant sort myself.

I was born Mary Posner in New York on September 19, 1920, and was abandoned to an orphanage. That is the beginning and end of what I know of my real parents, although the Communists were later to state with assurance that they were foreign-born. It was uncannily shrewd of them to know this, since I did not and do not.

My foster parents, my real parents so far as I am or ever will be concerned, adopted me from the orphanage in 1923, when I was two and a half. They were Ida and Harry Freed—my mother is still alive—and I became Marion Freed. My father was a clothier in Detroit then, but he and mother had taken to wintering in Miami and enjoying it so much that when I was barely four, we moved there. Father again opened his own haberdashery and in time we became affluent, on paper, in Coral Gables real estate. That was during the boom that became such a publicized bust. When it busted, so did we. I was nine then.

Father opened yet another store and got by for a third time. We never wanted, never once. I would say we were middle class. I was a child rich in devotion, an only child. The boy who would have been my brother if he had lived, Sherman Robert Freed, died of cancer at sixteen. It was after this tragedy that mother and father adopted me. Their capacity for parental love was enriched by their grief.

A Groundwork for Betrayal

There was a stunted colt of a cocoanut tree in our front yard in Miami when we moved there, and when we left in 1939 it was grown. That is my clearest way of measuring time then. The rest went by as the young years do. I went to primary school, then Miami Senior High, finally to the University of Miami. I was bright in the scholarly way: I graduated third in my class from the high school and *cum laude* from U. of M. I can find no significance there to the purpose of this book except that biographical needs must be served.

Very clearly, from the ages of six to sixteen, I remember that hurricanes were fun. I guess lots of things are until you get old enough to have an intelligent point of view and understand that fun has bounds of its own. Our hurricanes began with the winds and the warnings, the palms whipping and dipping more madly than usual like drunk old biddies with big hats. Then the gas and electricity would be shut off at the source, and the storm shutters set to ready, and candles and hurricane lamps lighted. There would be the house, half-dark, and the lunatic scream of the winds and none of it any more real than playing a game. The Indians were out there but they could never get at us: a fine sensation.

We always knew when the eye of the storm came, for it meant a twenty-minute or half-hour lull, and the kids were allowed out for as long as that. We'd play in the street nearby, banking the derelict fronds and being pleasantly awed by the bright, pouncing look of the sky, then go to cover again until the hurricane had finished its business and gone on to the Gulf of Mexico. The reports in the next day's papers were not real: so many million dollar's worth of damage, so many window panes, so many trees blown down. Well, of course trees were down. What would you expect of a hurricane? I don't recall much bodily injury.

My great love was—and is—music, the piano. I had studied it

since early childhood and later at the university gave lessons so that I could go on taking lessons. Mother and father gave me a white Steinway on my sixteenth birthday and it made that birthday unforgettable. It wasn't simply the fact of a piano, it was knowing too that in 1936 white Steinways didn't grow on trees—where, now that I think of it, they would have looked mighty silly.

When I entered the university the next year I had some scholarship aid. Scholastically I was, I have said, a trifle of an egghead. But life was well-rounded as well through all the student years. As a Miamian, I had the usual large quota of outdoor life and there were the usual parties and dates. Nothing can be gained or explained by any special reference to these, but I have not forgotten Harry Bast. Nor would Paul want me to.

He was my crush, a boy my age I met at the university. His mother and father had fled Russia in the early years of the Communist surge and Harry was born in steerage aboard the ship bound for this country. He went to classes days and studied nights and when he wasn't studying he was desk clerk at the hotel his parents had in Miami Beach. He studied and worked and clerked until he died from the aftermath of rheumatic fever. He was twenty-one. His last three months of life he was hopelessly bedridden. I wrote him daily till his death a week before Pearl Harbor.

After he died I had the first sustained depression I'd undergone since a summer in young teenage when nothing would relieve my spirits but eating in restaurants. Now there would be a war to overwhelm in time all the calamities that were irretrievable. And there was that, but again I boggle and digress, for there was no link in Harry's end to what came later. Bad men with Marxian dialectic did not kill Harry. Bacterial endocarditis did.

I had graduated from the university meanwhile and rejoined my parents in Jacksonville, where they had moved in 1939 during my junior year. I stayed in Miami to finish, but no longer. The stock market had done for father what Coral Gables had instituted and now he was making another start, with a shoe store. But by this time his chronic bronchitis had become severe to the point of having a more technical name and he was incapacitated a good deal of the time. The shoe store did not flourish. I helped somewhat by teaching primary grade school in West Riverside near Jax, as Jacksonville is locally known, and won some minor honors that may have indicated a capacity for leadership. One of these was in a Zionist organization. I mention it solely to show how malleable and directionless I still was. I was not a Zionist; it was just something to do.

And it still was going to be a long time before I conceived any hard and fast notions in regard to Communism. I had brushed against it vicariously in the way people do but had reserved conclusions, if any. As a matter of fact, I would have had a good word for the devil if he had tipped his hat. Mother and father were vaguely "against" Emma Goldman and what she stood for, but it was never clear to me what she did stand for. We were not so unsophisticated as to think in terms of men with beards, black hats and sputtering bombs but I, at least, was unsophisticated enough to know there were two sides to every question—and to consider myself highly sophisticated for so knowing.

Then again, Communism was not unfashionable in the 1930's. People were hungry and several intellectuals of high repute were chucking the Kremlin under the chin without being stoned for it. Some had dialectic enough to carry them through two cocktail parties without repeating themselves. I know now that they were no less dangerous for being silly but it was hard for anyone to perceive danger in a somewhat neurotic exhibitionism.

In fact, I knew a Communist of my own, a girl high school contemporary—and for those who might be inclined to be supercilious about that, may I say now and hurriedly that she *didn't* "get over it." She is today a hard-core Party worker in Los Angeles and as vicious a termite in the democratic structure as any I have met—and I have met hundreds.

She was not too bearable even then, an arrogant, ingrown beauty with plenty of money and a certain disdain for anyone who didn't walk around with *The New Yorker* under her arm. There are no typical Communists but there are Communist types. Marjorie, to give her a name that is not hers, was the snob Communist, of which there are many. It is a snobbery with directions of its own but each no less marked than the varieties we evoke ourselves. Marjorie's idea of damnation would be to be caught dead in the Stork Club clutching a *Saturday Evening Post*. Dead in the Automat with the *New Masses* is all right.

In Jacksonville in the fall of 1943 I met Paul Miller; or, let us say, a man named Paul Miller. Much of what I know now of his life then I was not to learn until later—some time, in fact, after we were married, and even today I have the feeling he has left patches untold. Repeatedly over the years he has made disclosures with the air of their being old hat to me, whereas I have not dreamed that this or that has happened to him. Seven years of Paul's life, beginning in 1939, were spent in undercover anti-Communist work for the FBI, as were five more when I too became a spy. But I surely did not know at that time nor even faintly suspect that he was allied with the Bureau as a card-carrying member of the Communist Party. I was to hear vague rumors in time of a possible Communist connection, but never was there a hint that he was a counter agent. He himself would not intimate it even when to have done so might have saved him some trouble. To this day I cannot help wondering if he might have confided in me if our marriage had hinged on his doing so—and to this day I do not know, because he doesn't either.

I met him at a USO party at a girl's home in Jax. Paul was an oiler in the Merchant Marine, which meant he was ashore—on the beach, as he said—for three or four weeks at a time. He was not at all my Hollywood-trained conception of a counterspy, which would be a tight-lipped enigmatic fellow. He was bubbling, talkative, more brash than most young men I knew and a little forward in what I can best describe as a backward way. I mean by that that Paul's romantic approach was dashing and pawing until they let the gate down. Then he became a blushing haykicker. But at first he struck me as a pretty piratical sort. I was pleasantly apprehensive.

Not till years later did I know that three months before we met, he had risked death from a drunken Russian officer in the desert country of Iran. Since Russia was our military ally then, I must add swiftly that it would have been in self-defense. I did not know nor did I care that Jacksonville was the central Communist station between New York and Chicago and Miami—and that within weeks of the night we met, Paul would be secretary of the Jacksonville Party. I did not dream he was on first-name terms with a few home-grown Reds so prominent that even I, one of the laity, had heard of them. I did not know that he danced well.

I understand now that my knowledge of what he had gone through influenced my own choice of action when the time came. That much I will have to say was a definite link, though I like to think I would have done the same on my own initiative. But I was years in evaluating what he had done and been willing to do. Even after my first comprehension of his role in this battle of free men, I was not impressed by the Communist threat and had a fleeting thought that Paul had been going to too many movies. Still it is apparent at last that Marion Miller, apprentice spy, did not evolve wholly from a magic puff of dust. Psychologists will be relieved to know that there *were* connective factors.

It would be wrong to overstate Paul, as he is the first to admit —and criminal to understate him. He is a romantic and his fantasies were swashbucklers. They still are. But beyond these, he is fiercely a patriot and more fiercely than that a free man. His values, so much more intense than those of us who accept priceless treasure as an inevitable heritage, are rooted in the memories of want and pain. His grandparents, to whom he was so deeply devoted, emigrated from Poland. Their knowledge of oppression was very much first-hand, like their knowledge of anti-Semitism. They were orthodox and devout. They did not live under Communism, but they had the old country's wisdom of what it portended and what it was doing. White Fascism was not vastly different than Red. They desperately hated and feared the new manifesto. They dreaded the amused cynicism they saw around them, regarding it, a young American dismissal of it, as something that would have its droll moment and go away. They instilled their feeling in Paul. It was the same with his mother and father, although the profound instincts of the grandparents affected him more. So Paul, you see, is not merely Jack Armstrong. He is the legitimate heir of a tradition ancient in its enmity to being pushed around.

That is the great fundamental as Paul sees it. I suspect he's a little shaky on the fine print of Marxian economics but it is not clear to him, nor to me, why anyone would have to understand *Das Kapital* to loathe Communism. *Das Kapital* is bewildering, and mighty sticky going even where it isn't—but who cannot see what has grown out of it? We all understand, because it has been spelled out for us by the Communists themselves, that the first condition of the Communist state is the subjugation of parliamentary law, also known as democracy, also known as the will of the people. If this end is accomplished, the rest is academic and nothing to bother the economic detractors of Karl Marx, since they will then think as they are told to think or—else. To argue that Communist theory is nonsense is itself nonsense, inasmuch as that is not the issue. The issue is the death struggle over enforcement, and that is here and it is now. That is what Paul was fighting on the field. That is what I fought.

Paul was born in Chicago and raised in Providence, Rhode Island. There was not money to put him through high school or the luxury of part-time employment, so he became a poster artist when scarcely more than a boy, serving his apprenticeship in burlesque theaters. Burlesque, I am told, had its troubles, and Paul traveled south on the wave of the depression. I should say the riptide. In Jacksonville he set up shop—the plot coalesces suddenly—in the same office building that housed the National Maritime Union. Paul became friendly with some of its local officials and one of these one day, having tested his ground for a number of weeks, told my husband-to-be that he was a fool not to join the Communist Party. It was the argument of this man, an Anglo-Italian still fighting deportation, that by so doing Paul would accomplish three desirable ends: (1) stay out of the shooting war that was sure to come; (2) be a member of the Communist hierarchy that would be running the world any day now, and (3) do the American CP a lot of good.

Paul's first reaction was the go-to-hell reflex, his second more considered. He told the recruiter, that he'd think it over. Next day he went to the FBI offices in Jacksonville and talked to a man there named Rudolph Alt, a veteran who had come into the Bureau along with J. Edgar Hoover. The scenario grows a little murky here due to Paul's reticence, but the upshot ultimately was that the Bureau would be pleased to have Paul's aid, and did he understand entirely what he was doing? That was to say that should anything unpleasant occur, the Bureau could not easily come to his rescue, if at all. He understood.

For the year after he met me Paul had nothing on his mind but the Bureau, the Communists, the Merchant Marine and his courtship. Of these, I think the last was the least complicated of his problems. Fortunately for his peace of mind, I did not doubt for long my feeling for Paul and I did not waste time in disseminating. Thus, when after four months or so we became formally engaged, Paul did not have to be anxious over whom I might be seeing when he was at sea. He *was* anxious but I could not help that. I could help, on the other hand, his feeling about his engine room duties, which was not happy. I gave him no ultimatums but did say that if he were going to do his duty in the service to which he was committed, he would be no less functional doing it under pleasanter circumstances. It was surely not out of the question that Paul should become an officer.

To this end he was assigned to training school in New London, Connecticut, in the summer of 1944. At the same time I went to Washington as a typist in the War Department. Some aspects of officer training, particularly those having to do with physics, almost drove Paul mad but he got through and joined me in Washington on the last day of August. We returned to Jacksonville immediately and were married there September 3. We had a week's honeymoon in Charleston before Paul shipped out again. Now he was an engine officer, gentleman by courtesy of the merchant marine and the Communist Party, whose permission he had to have to put in for training in the first place. The Communists are not insouciant about those things. But they did always want, it seemed, a member of officer rank on each ship if such a placement were possible, for purposes of party liaison with the crew.

From this run it did not seem Paul would ever get home, but he did; and four times again after that, and then the war was over. But so, it appeared, was the poster business in the state of Florida. Its resurgence in Jacksonville, at any rate, was terribly slow and Paul terribly restless. During his early service with the Merchant Marine, he had spent some time in Hawaii and fallen in love with it. Now, he said, he would leave me for as long as it took to establish certain connections in Honolulu; then I would join him there and we would live happily ever after.

Leaving Jax, he also severed his connections with the Communist Party as well as, presumably, with the FBI. He did it with almost implausible simplicity—just left town without telling the CP. This, too, I heard about later. I do know that no one ever bothered me or asked me a single question.

Paul got as far as Los Angeles by train, sitting up day and night and subsisting on bologna sandwiches and root beer. He did not get any further. Just one of those things. Friends and relatives there steered him to poster artist firms who assured him the business was thriving. It was. Everything was. In a week Paul had a job at more money than he had ever before been paid weekly, and a month later I was with him. We were home.

I have a word for something in accounts like these, a distant cousin to irrelevant name-dropping called the dud-bomb. It is when the writer mentions out of hand some episode that would seem to have the promise of explosive, then simply walks away from it to leave it ticking away there forever. I see I have done that already, leap-frogging glibly over the mention that on one hegira Paul was nearly shot to death by a Russian officer. I will rectify my omission now. I think that Paul's account of the incident might be read with profit by quite a few Americans.

It began in the early summer of 1943, when Paul engaged the trail of a Communist whom he suspected of being a courier and, for at least this particular voyage, a courier with a message of importance to someone high in Kremlin circles. By means of his own, Paul arranged to be a fellow-crewman of this man and was able to follow him from Basra harbor in Iran into the interior. There the man slipped away, so in a sense Paul's mission had failed. Yet its aftermath must have given the Bureau some fascinating moments.

From the port of Basra, the men of the S.S. *Thomas J. Jarvis* were given leave, and Paul and his Communist affiliate joined a hunting party upcountry. Paul is a good shot but a half-hearted hunter. There were reasons nonetheless for not stepping out of a character he had created for himself so on an early expedition he winged a running gazelle, the leader of a herd. The gazelle contributed the wrenching shock of element of looking back as it was hit, its brute eyes full for an instant of astounding inquiry, and dying of what clearly was nothing but heartbreak. Paul still has the head.

It was the next morning that Paul's Communist quarry disappeared from the tent they shared, not to be seen again. With nothing more to be done about that, Paul continued with the rest of the party north to the transfer point the Soviet army had set up to receive its lend-lease equipment from us; in effect, a matériel dump into which this day were being transported locomotives and similar heavy equipment from the *Jarvis* and other ships.

In charge of the Russian detachment was a Soviet officer with a name pronounced as though it might be spelled Steranov in English, wearing on his shoulders the insignia of a full colonel and on his left breast ribboned whorls which meant nothing to most of the Americans. Steranov, Paul remembers, was a good-looking man with the face of a British pukka sahib and beautiful Oxonian English to go with it. He explained he had British tutors in his home in a Moscow suburb. His rank precluded, it seems, his mingling with anyone of military status, mostly his own men, but he gravitated toward Paul, who wore civilian clothes and was therefore outside the strictures of caste. Steranov had a good deal of tough charm and presently, when he invited Paul to join him in a drive even further north to the improvised Soviet base, Paul accepted. It occurred to him that something of use might be gained, though certainly he could not have guessed what.

The distance from the transfer dump to the base was twenty-odd miles along a "road," Paul said later, that might have been paved by negligent shell-fire. They drove it in Steranov's jeep, the product of that sturdy Soviet city, Detroitograd, Michigan. Of the tents that were on the base, Steranov had by far the best, though it amounted to nothing more than a canvas trap for the incredible heat. Steranov beckoned Paul in and left the flap open, conceding that much to man's need to breathe. He threw the switch keys carelessly on the table, excused himself brusquely, and went to open a bottle of vodka. Steranov, it developed shortly, was in a mood not simply to drink but to get drunk. And so he did.

Paul himself is not much of a drinker but he had learned the device of mouthing liquor while swallowing, and hiding a glass's contents behind a closed hand. This trick of deception involves mainly being able to spit the mouth's contents back into a handkerchief behind the sound of coughing, and becomes easier as one's vis-a-vis becomes drunker. In not very much time, abetted by the heat, Steranov had a skinful; he was, as Paul says, a full colonel and no mistake. As the bottle's level dropped, he became ugly in temper without giving immediate notice of the fact. It was all a kind of mottled silence. Finally he rapped the table sharply and said a word so utterly out of context with what had been going on that Paul was startled into witlessness.

"Stupid," said Steranov gently.

"Comrade?" Paul is sure today there was real alarm in his tone, the alarm he would reserve for a barroom buddy who suddenly turned vicious. His surprise was justified—he had confided to Steranov at great length his American Communist affiliation and been received with much alcoholic sympathy. When Steranov said nothing further, Paul asked: "Are you speaking of me—your friend?"

"Of you—my friend," Steranov muttered. "Very funny. You, my stupid friend." He poured himself another drink. "I've been sitting here wondering if I should tell you something, and I have decided yes. I assure you it will make no difference either way."

Both his words and manner were ominous enough to give Paul some degree of comfort in having his service revolver tucked beneath his jacket in his belt. Steranov wore his own pistol in a holster by his side. For want of anything better to say, Paul said:

"Well—I'll be glad to hear."

"No," said Steranov, "you won't be glad to hear." Sweat was soaking his tunic by then, staining the queer red insignia. "You know," he went on to Paul, "who I am? All right, all right, a man named Steranov. But do you know *what* I am?"

"Why—yes. My friend, the colonel."

"Your friend, yes. Ah, my stupid, stupid friend. I am a commissar, Miller stupid. You know what a commissar is? A political detachment to watch over the military for deviates. No. deviationists. Of course you know. I am a Communist, Miller, like yourself, but a *Russian* Communist. Master Communist. The masters and the architects of the new world. You understand that?"

"Yes. The world of deliverance. We Communists in America embrace you." Unconsciously Paul had adapted himself to Steranov's formal syntax.

"Good," said Steranov. "It's nice of you to think that way. Because when we Russians come to ultimate power—and I do not mean Communist Internationale or anything so Utopian as that —we will rule your country. And oh, my friend, what plans we have for you!"

"I know. I know!"

Steranov began to laugh, saliva on the corners of his mouth. "You know, you know. You know like hell. I am going to tell you something, and please remember you are listening to a commissar. Elite, believe me. Overseer. To put it another way—*you* don't know. *I* know."

"Yes, colonel. "

" 'Yes, colonel.' Then do you know this—when we come to the States, we Russians, when we are your rulers, who will be the first to go, the very first? Who? Tell me."

"Why, the capitalist hogs, the exploiters—"

"No! I knew you would say it. These, they have some of the qualities we can respect, any enemy whose strength we can turn to our own use. The gift and the habit of authority, not bad foremen. No. The first to go will be the American Communists! Every last one."

This was educational. Paul's jaw dropped without the need for pretense. "But, comrade! Why? *I* am a Communist. We're brothers."

"You then, brother. You with the rest, though we need not wait for them, you and I. You want to know why, you who know everything? Because you are traitors to your own, your own country, your own people. Your government. It stinks but it's yours. Do you think for a minute we will trust you? Think! If traitors to American rule, why not to Russian? You're garbage, the lot of you. We have always known it. We will never forget it. Number One on our list."

He subsided into a kind of lip-smacking darkness of his own. Paul did not speak, having run out of any words worth more than two kopeks.

"And after these," Steranov went on after a moment, "the Jews. Every Jew."

Paul turned sideways and braced both feet, his weight forward. "But I am a Jew. And here we sit and drink together."

"Enjoy it, Jew. Enjoy your drink. Make every moment count. You have deep religious ties, do you not? Even if you are not yourself religious. In the Catholic way. So we have made arrangements for you both. Haven't we set the record clear enough, for all you fools like yourselves to see? How can we abide you? The answer is, we cannot."

"Then why do you tell me this?"

Steranov didn't bother to answer. Indeed, the answer was nearly self-evident. "Now listen," he said instead. "You will find the program of liquidation fascinating. After the religions, the labor unions. Millions more lives. Terrible, isn't it? You find me ludicrous perhaps, but you will learn—or would if you ever left this tent, which is the first and last joke you will hear from me."

Well, he is ludicrous in retrospect. Dialogue like Steranov's was bad enough to do nicely for the daytime television of now. But nobody felt funny, Paul the lesser of the two.

"We have ways," said Steranov, "of crushing out millions of lives. Millions, literally. We taught the Germans how, not they us. And we have learned more since. The unionists cannot survive, and for one very good reason. They have been taught to be-lieve in the dignity of labor. A noble phrase—but in itself im-practical. No more can we permit you Jews and Catholics your devotions or even your atavisms. Not in a rightly atheistic society. You're thinking we pay lip service to the proletariat and you are right. But for a good reason. If you were a thinking man, you would know it. But you are not a thinking man. You are a dirty, lousy American Communist, a fool and a would-be fouler of your own nest. You are useful to us for now, taken all together, but you Miller-stupid, you are all of a sudden dispen-sable. Oh, very."

He drank the last of the vodka from the bottle rather than his glass and set the bottle back with great care. In movies I'm sure he would have thrown it, on top of all that bottle-throwing ver-biage, but Steranov evidently stepped out of character at the wrong times.

"Ah, Miller," Steranov went on, "what a book you could write if ever you were going home again. You think now we are devils, but we are not. We are sensible men and that is all. So at last you have heard us—are you through with your stupid dream?"

Not until that second, Paul believes now, did he have his first real awareness of how grim actually had been his distrusts. There had been in him, even as he served the Bureau, the thin residue of a feeling that even Satan would not destroy his own. But this dread sentence he was hearing was not merely the regurgitation of a grandiose sot, a flatulent ham, but rather—if Steranov could be believed—the voice of Soviet policy. He did not know and cannot guess what accessibility Steranov may in fact have had to the Kremlin. But his tongue had the sound of authoritative as-surance.

And still Paul made an effort to confirm what he feared. Stera-nov had talked so much, he might talk a little more.

"How am I," asked Paul, "to believe all this? Will Comrade Stalin verify it?"

Steranov's eyes, which had gone away again, returned to the tent and one fateful instant of bare and drunken dedication.

"That," he said, "you'll never know. Goodbye, you son of a bitch." And he reached for his gun.

So the end would come, Paul thought—derring-do, as in murder fiction, but unlike murder fiction, with knowledge unfulfilled. In well brought-up books, the killer tells all before he gets his comeuppance. He talks, he babbles like a man obsessed or, in any event, one who has made a solemn compact with the author. Steranov had not obliged.

But in that moment of all-or-nothing, he did obey another dictate of fiction. His gun caught on its holster. Paul's behaved splendidly. So there was Steranov, a sitting duck, his expression for a split second that of a host whose guest had vomited on the rug. Then he said: "But you cannot shoot. My men are everywhere."

And it was true. Shooting the colonel would have been a high-priced luxury indeed. Not shooting him, on the other hand, would have seemed ridiculous.

Paul said, "Now where are we?"

Steranov said, "Drop your gun." His tone had become pleasant. "Don't be silly."

"Drop your gun," said Steranov. "You may yet live. Who knows?"

Paul has a gift of debatable value: he thinks fast. Over the span of a lifetime, it has got him into more trouble than it's worth, since it has got him out of the habit of thinking twice. But on this day, it was a godsend.

Lowering but not dropping his gun, he said: "You must let me go. I have something to give you. Not you, but the glorious cause we both serve. You're right—I may yet live. And so may you."

"What are you talking about?"

Paul said: "Like the animal you are, you wanted to kill me. Now for a change, think like the Communist you are instead of the animal. You have sat here and told me the true aims of the Kremlin. Wouln't it serve your ends to have me tell my countrymen of what awaits them? Stop and reflect—Americans would be paralyzed into submission by this knowledge."

Steranov stared. "Or into fighting till death. I never heard your countrymen were cowards."

"No. Because your terms would not mean the end of those of us whose word is law. They would be even stronger. When I say paralyzed, I mean that our rulers would create the paralysis. They would make submission sound entirely logical. Then you may strike at your ease and your will."

Steranov pinched his lower lip. "You would have to wait till after the war. We are your beloved allies now, don't forget."

"I would wait."

Steranov sighed. "If I let you go," he said, "it is for two reasons. One, you are a true Communist and may just be speaking the truth. The other, that you have the gun. But I can't understand your agreeing to propagandize for your own death warrant. You know you would be among the first to go because I've told you so."

"As you said, I am a true Communist."

"But such sacrifice—!"

"And as you also said, I have the gun."

"Ah. Spoken like one of us. Now I *believe* you are a true Communist. I say this to you, though: forget what you have promised me and we'll find you wherever you are. You understand, Americans won't believe you anyway. They don't care or think about us. But what have I to lose?"

"I won't forget."

Nor has he forgotten. Paul has said to many others the words of Steranov as they are told here.

"You're a lucky man," said Steranov. "Get to your feet. Take the car keys from the table. Leave the jeep at the dump."

"Hand me your gun first. Butt pointed toward me."

"What if I don't?"

"I'll take a chance on getting away. Over your dead body. That's an American expression, in a way."

Steranov staggered upright and put his hands above his head. "Take it yourself."

He made no other move. Paul scooped up the keys and drove Detroit's lend-lease vehicle back to the dump. There was no pursuit nor a sign of it. Maybe Steranov always turned over his jeep to visitors after cocktails. In a week Paul sailed away from Basra and in a few more weeks was at a USO party in Jacksonville, where he met Marion Freed.

Thus it was—or thus it almost was. For his part, Paul never has wholly recovered from that trip. It disturbs his sleep from time to time and always will. He is better since putting the gazelle's head out of sight but the knowledge of the one betrayal always will haunt him.

If he had it to do over, he says today, he would not have murdered that wild, free thing that died for no reason, in the world made by God.

Our first years in Los Angeles, beginning in 1947, were happy and uneventful and I cannot say how fitfully the spewings and violent threats of Colonel Steranov kicked in my subconscious, or as much of the story as Paul ever has told me. Not very fitfully, I suspect. In time Paul set up his business independently and it went well. I am a joiner and joined organizations furiously. One led to another, as they have a way of doing, and a third group to a fourth.

And by and by I received in the mail one day in 1950 an invitation to attend a conference of the Los Angeles Committee for Protection of Foreign Born. It struck me as an oddly bad-tempered summons, full of inveighing against the McCarran Act, but other than that it meant nothing. I was on the point of throwing it away when Paul asked to see it. His trained eye detected immediately the jargon of a Communist front, the yowling and intemperate abuse these people lean to. An old fear and restlessness stirred within him. I hated to see it happen. I didn't care the way he did. But the words of Colonel Steranov must have come back from somewhere.

"This meeting," Paul said, giving me back the invitation. "I think you should go to it. There'd be a reason."

"What reason?" I really didn't have to ask.

He spread his hands. "We can all help," he said, "a little bit. Let's anyway see what the Bureau thinks about it."

"The FBI?" Even with my knowledge of his past, it all sounded gaudy and improbable.

"Who else? They're in the phone book, you know. Will you let me call them?"

We have ways, said Steranov out of the past, of crushing out millions of lives. Millions, literally. Masters, rulers.

"I'll call them," I said.

And I did.

3

Enter Mrs. Miller

NOW IT WAS AUTUMN OF 1950. ESTHER AVENUE sprawled dozing in Indian summer. Outside a little boy fell off his tricycle and got up and righted it without crying. Such a ridiculous climate to set in motion the years-long night of terror and intrigue.

My "summons" from the Los Angeles Committee for Protection of Foreign Born lay before me. The return address on the envelope identified the organization as part of the Civil Rights Congress. Its date was October 5. As I dialed the Bureau's number, I felt very much like a spinster about to insist to police there was a man under her bed.

Despite Paul's experience and misgivings, I could *not* take this thing seriously, any more than one believes in the face of overwhelming evidence that one's neighbor is a sought-after cat burglar. Friends of mine that year had had a warm acquaintance with a man across the street from them, a charming Britisher, who one night was arrested for having relieved Beverly Hills homes of thousands of dollars worth of jewelry. They knew he couldn't have done it. But he had. Truth is not stranger than fiction in context or construction. It is stranger only because it *does* happen to be the truth.

The man I finally talked to at the Bureau was a warm and wonderful fellow named Ed White, today head of personnel for an aircraft company near Los Angeles and still one of my dearest friends. He did not laugh at me or sound bored or peremptory. Bureau men are not very chatty on a telephone but he asked to come and see me next day. I agreed because there was nothing else to do—I had hoped and rather supposed that he would say thank you and now go somewhere and drop dead. I have been described in later years as a heroine, but I am not a heroine. They are made of sterner and gaudier stuff.

That night after dinner, one I could scarcely eat and not taste at all, I re-read my "summons." It seemed angry and intemperate as ever but I did not take on meaning until Paul read it aloud, underscoring the passages that had raised his hackles as the scent of danger will raise the hackles of a wary and veteran beast. To reprint it in its entirety is, I think, apropos. You will see for yourself, indoctrinated as we are in this new decade, the swatches of Communist lexicon that only now are they learning to control.

It was titled grandly "A Call to a Los Angeles Conference to Defend the Rights of Foreign Born"—laudable enough on the face of it. It urged that I and other recipients "mobilize for action to defeat the deportation drive, concentration camp laws and revocation of citizenship"—in short, to help sink the recently born McCarran Act, which in effect was directed at alien Communist infiltration. Its day was the following Sunday, October 8, its time one to five p.m. for delegates and observers. That night it would be converted to a reception for the executive secretary for the American Committee for Protection of Foreign Born.

Actually, as I was shortly to learn, the Bureau's immediate objective was to prove an affiliation of the Los Angeles committee with the American, or national, committee, since this last had already been set down in Washington as a Communist front. At this juncture the Los Angeles committee plainly was not denying such an affiliation, although in a very few weeks time they were going to disavow any connection whatever. Nonetheless, proof was lacking. This was where Marion Miller came in.

The place of the meeting was Parkview Manor in downtown Los Angeles.

Passing over italics and a rather fancy job of typesetting, this is what the summons said and the words in which it said it:

"Who but fascist-minded demagogues would deny the right of foreign-born citizens and residents of the United States to think and act like free-born men and women?" (The McCarran Act, which set up immigration quotas, clearly was interpreted by Communists as a deliberate buffer against their continued growth here and their right to booby-trap the electorate. I'm sure they were correct; the late Senator Pat McCarran of Nevada must have had precisely that in mind.)

"In the years before the 'cold war' was launched, it was possible to read such dignified official pronouncements as that of Supreme Court Justice Frank Murphy who, in June, 1945, said:

"'But once an alien lawfully enters and resides in this country he becomes invested with the rights guaranteed by the Constitution to all people within our borders. Such rights include those protected by the First and Fifth Amendments and by the due process clause of the Fourteenth Amendment. None of these provisions acknowledges any distinction between citizens and resident aliens.'

[53]

"Today many more than 150 persons are being threatened with deportation, which means forced separation from their families, for exercising their rights to think freely and belong to trade unions, political parties, fraternal and cultural organizations of their own choosing. And the Justice Department, aided by current fascist-like legislation, threatens to proceed against thousands of citizens and non-citizens with deportation warrants, revocation of citizenship of the foreign-born, and concentration camps.

"Many of these cases are current in the Los Angeles area, notorious also for mass deportations of Mexican field workers when seasonal requirements have run their course.

"This monstrous situation is the result of deliberate propaganda by the war-makers and architects of the police-state, who spread lies and slander about the foreign-born, radicals and minority peoples, in order to confuse and divide the American people so that rights of citizens and non-citizens to freedom of thought and association can be destroyed.

"The Immigration Service of the Justice Department, operating in its official sphere of oppression, says to some three million foreign-born non-citizens: Think as we dictate, do as we say—or we will deport you! To millions of naturalized citizens it repeats this warning, threatening revocation of citizenship.

"Legislators, local and national, finding 'justification' in the hysteria they have fostered over the years, pass fascist-like laws saying in effect to citizens and non-citizens alike:

"Submit to our will, consent to our policies, stop fighting for peace, progress, and trade union rights, or we will put you in concentration camps!

"Although many American people are dazed and confused by the constant barrage of lies, hate, and war propaganda, they are basically democratic in their outlook. They must be made aware that their own heritage of freedom is being undermined by denial of rights to the foreign-born.

"History has shown us that deportations can be prevented, and that oppressive legislation can be defeated or, once enacted, can be wiped off the statute books by determined popular activity.

"We therefore invite all organizations and individuals to join with us in the discussion of the current attack on the rights of foreign-born citizens and non-citizens, and the planning of action."

Pretty turgid going, isn't it? But the sheen of myopic logic is there, the logic of the propagandist. As the producer of a play may twist a critical review to his own ends for advertisement purposes, using the words he needs and nothing more, so these people had presented an argument in sophistry. Paul saw it. I didn't. I was still busy being liberal. In Paul's reading it aloud after dinner, it lost some of its turgid quality, but I was still beginning to wish I hadn't consented to see Ed White. I was busy enough with my own life. Paul, Jr. was a little boy, Betsy an infant. There was a house to keep up. Furthermore, I held to a fairly prevalent view that Communists, even if such they were, were no more a menace to the American way of life than bisons, and probably not much more numerous. "Anyway, what makes you think they're Communists?"

"How can you miss it?" said Paul. "Who else talks about fascists and concentation camps? Not Democrats. Not Republicans. Not even Socialists." Paul was excited. He had been too many years out of the world of Walter Mitty. He wanted back in again. And I had to remember that he was a militant rather than a passive patriot. But the "invitation," should you want to call it that, had come to me. I wondered in passing how I had got on a mailing list of a group so ready to foam at the mouth, but I supposed they had picked me from the roster of one of my other clubs. (They had: Pioneer Women of America.) I also wondered, as perhaps you would have: Why me? In time I found that out too. They needed a badge of respectability as well as a possible wedge into other and conservative non-suspect organizations. Pioneer Women would have given them a fine cover. But now suddenly I was only tired and irritable.

"You see Communists under the bed," I told Paul. "Why don't you forget them?"

"They are under the bed," he said. "As for forgetting them, they'd love that, in the sense you mean. If they could get enough like me to forget them, they'd have very nice sailing. Too nice."

"And what do you want me to do? After all, the FBI is paid for this. And we do have a military intelligence and I'd imagine an espionage service."

"I imagine. But not enough to go around. There's never enough. The Bureau will tell you that."

"And what about Paul and Betsy? Do we let them forage for left-over salami while I'm out saving the world? My first duty is to you and the children. And to myself. If that's selfish, I'm selfish."

"I could answer that, but I won't. Besides, I can look after the children. You have a duty to civilization, too. I'm not impugning your patriotism. I just know what I know."

"Honey, can't you ever forget Jacksonville?"

"No. At least, I hope not. Anyway, it's only for a day. That can't hurt anything."

"A day," I said. "Spying on a bunch of people that make

sense in their own eyes, and not a bit of proof they're Communists."

"They're Communists or Communist-directed. Take my word for it. Or if you don't like that, take Ed White's word when he comes."

"Ed White's word! I thought the FBI never evaluated their findings. I thought if they found a man with a smoking gun standing over a person just shot to death, they wouldn't even make a guess as to what happened. I thought . . ."

"That's the law," said Paul. "But the law doesn't compel them to be blind. In fact, they have better eyes and ears than most and we ought to thank God for it. I don't want to remind you again about Steranov."

"You don't have to. That's why I called. But all the way downtown, and on a Sunday—our day to be together, all of us. Not even a concert would get me down there, not Horowitz. And to sneak around a lot of pathetic people—"

"I'm not very touched," said Paul. "Neither will you be once you see the pattern. One day, that's all. One day."

One day—and it grew into five years. They were years of strain and agony and a little boredom. But I wouldn't want them back and I never ask myself why? I know why. And I will always know they were the five years I gave to my country. We go on giving, Paul and I, as a result of them. We are invited to lecture now on what we have done, sometimes as often as twenty-one days or nights a month, and people do listen to us and it has given my life a meaning it would never have had otherwise.

Ed White was a wonderful guy. He still is. He came out the next day and we sat talking for an hour or two. At intervals I burped two-months-old Betsy, who was slung over my shoulder like grain. A not very dramatic setting but Ed was pleased with it, as he told me later. The FBI had successfully planted other dilettante workers with the Communist apparatus but none, I believe, as innocuous and yet, to the Reds, more credible than I. I am sure of this: I have never known to this day who the other operatives were, and they know of me only because I came to the attention of the public. The Bureau wants it this way. But I do know that the Party embraced and trusted me from the beginning; much more than they should have. I even understand why their bitterness and hatred was that much more intense when I testified for the Government. I understand but I am not remorseful; if my ethical standards have taken a beating, then it was in a good cause.

Ed didn't cajole that day, or browbeat, or wave the flag or do anything he shouldn't have done. He explained the situation in the role of friend to friend. He conveyed to me the terrible importance of spotlighting Communists wherever they might be. He noted the absence of proof that the Los Angeles Committee for Protection of Foreign Born was in fact part of the national body, although assuredly it was. He pinpointed my assignment: to gather such proof.

That was my job really, from first to last. I never did undergo adventures as woolly as those of our friend Herbert Philbrick. I did not meet shadowy characters or Kremlin brass in Vienna and Moscow, in the manner of Mr. Boris Morros. I did not need the total moral fiber of Matt Cvetic, whose mother died thinking he was a Red. I did infiltrate the Communist Party of the United States more thoroughly than I'd ever dreamed I might—and very shortly after my first meeting, at that. And in so doing, I did supply links and incidental information that may yet prove invaluable.

In all that time, I risked mainly only two things: my status as a social human being and my life. But I do not resent those risks; I gained a whole new perspective and became a whole person.

Of course, I agreed to do as Ed White asked. It is not easy to forget that first meeting, even while nothing of a pyrotechnic nature occurred. I drove downtown to what is now MacArthur Park, climbed a flight of steps to a shabby meeting hall, and sat on a folding chair, as people do in meetings all over the world. I was frightened and sure that I wore the word SPY stenciled on my back, but nobody seemed to notice.

The people were friendly enough. I was convinced by now that this certainly was a Communist front, but after looking around, I felt only a sense of disbelief and unreality. So these were the bogeymen and the bogeywomen, the dread Communists themselves! They did not for the most part look fearsome. They looked a bit raggedy, as though their incomes were extremely modest, and some had an unbathed appearance. They were evidently about sixty per cent foreign born, and I found in my later experience that three-quarters of them were active Communists, perhaps ten per cent hard core. Men and women— women in greater number.

I had been briefed only roughly on what to seek so I doodled on a pad and took sketchy but copious notes behind the doodling. (I would learn by and by that note-taking is not advisable at Communist group meetings. I explained it away this time by saying I wished to make a report to my own clubs. That pleased them—once.) The woman next to me was a handsome, well-groomed middle-aged person I shall call Josephine. Throughout, she knitted industriously. I, too, had my knitting with me and it gave us a bond. I would know Josephine better; she was hard-core.

The speakers stuck by and large to the announced agenda.

They were real mad at Senator McCarran. Each seemed madder than the one before. One guest of honor was I think maddest of all. But there was a purpose to all this ire. It was to raise money for the defense of certain comrades already up for deportation. One of the announced contributions was from the Communist Party, local branch. Beyond that, the word Communist was employed rarely and never significantly. But the climate of Communism was in every word and act. I stayed to the end.

I don't think that on that day anything more stimulating than intellectual curiosity moved me. I disapproved of Communism as one disapproves of barracuda, but the exercise of hearing what Satan had to say for himself was most exciting. Meanwhile, Josephine and I got quite a lot of knitting done.

I must say it was a lovely day. That seemed strange somehow. Beyond this stuffy hall and its undercurrent of trembling rage and violence, there was the sound of birds, and children playing in the park. Lightning and distant thunder would have been more appropriate.

I drove home in the dusk and had a light dinner, dutifully reported to Paul, and wrote out my findings for the FBI. It took me till three in the morning, and I had no idea if I had anything or not.

But I must have had. Months afterward, I was told that my report roused the suspicions of the Bureau—against me. My report had struck them as entirely too thorough not to be the work of a professional, and there was a school of thought that the Communists had planted a member in FBI ranks—one who called herself Marion Miller!

When I had finished and mailed the report, I slept like a child. I had done my duty and that was that.

That wasn't that. I had just begun.

4

If It Quacks Like a Duck

BUT IF THE ELABORATENESS OF MY MAIDEN REPOR-
torial effort had roused suspician among certain elements, my
earnest comportment at the meeting had served a better end. My
new friend Josephine, who was an influential member of the committee, reported favorably on me to her associates, and they accepted without much argument my explanation that I had taken
notes for transmittal to my own clubs.

That was one side of the coin. The other was that psychologically I was hooked from the beginning. There was more of
Paul in me than I had suspected. The conspiratorial framework
of what I was doing excited me, yes. But that wasn't the main
thing. The main thing was that I did sense the aura of danger,
real danger, from the outset. That one meeting, with its climate
of invective and hatred, its badly reasoned bitterness toward
constituted authority, was enough to dispel my laissez-faire—
which in the beginning had amounted to cynicism. These people wanted to do damage and they could do damage. The day
after, I awoke in such a torment of apprehension that I wanted
to shout my discovery up and down the gentle undulations of

Esther Avenue. But nobody would have cared, or not much of anybody. And someone *had* to care.

Well, all right. Circumstances had nominated me. Our lives do not change direction easily. Any fundamental diversion from course is a violent wrench. This was. But I say again that I am glad. Many things that happened I look back on in terror and sadness. But if I had to do it over—you know the rest of that line.

There were more conferences with Special Agent Ed White, and it was decided I would become ostensibly a convert to the Communist program, playing it all by ear, seeing how thoroughly I could penetrate the apparatus, and make it all a full-time project. Evidently the Bureau's misgivings had dissolved.

Paul was a trifle wild with frustration. It was a glorious chance to be Jack Armstrong again but his mild and non-flamboyant wife had got the part. Naturally there were good reasons for this. Paul had faded away from Jacksonville without a word, the sort of disappearance not well tolerated by Communists, and there was always the chance—thin as it might be—that he would be recognized at some future meeting. His garrulous contention—Paul can talk his way in or out of anything—that he could and would convert such recognition into an asset finally was acceded to, but he never did win more than a supporting role.

My very quietness and apparent sincerity were just what the Bureau wanted and needed in the part, besides the fact that I was a woman. The Communists, on the other hand, wanted me for related reasons: I dressed well and conservatively, made my points with a low voice and the disciplined force of education, and bathed at least once a day. There were times when they doubted me and even times when they suspected me of planned treachery, but I could allow myself the frail comfort of knowing they suspected everyone, most of all one another.

In time the Bureau gave heed to Paul's arguments and he joined me at many group meetings. Within months we both became registered Communists, he for the second time, and this was a great stride forward. But lest you think the whole experience was a prolonged lark, let me say that it was not. It was deadly serious, full of gnawing tensions, and it remains so to this day. Paul derived some exhilaration from it because that's how he is, but we never did form the habit of tickling one another in a delirium of joy. It's not that kind of game.

Communists are a suspicious and cautious lot. They have to be. Their system of checks and espionage is elaborate and all their devices to escape detection that seem childish are not childish in the least. To call them so would be to underrate the Bureau. But they have a naïveté of their own and one aspect of it is traceable to their theory of unquestioning obedience. If higher-ups approve of accepting this person or that as reliable, underlings do not argue the decision. Indeed they'd better not.

Within weeks of my first meeting, and after I had attended several more, I had a call from the downtown office of the Foreign Born Committee. Its content was nearly unbelievable. They wished me to serve as office secretary—to all intents and purposes, recording secretary. They might have done worse by appointing J. Edgar Hoover their chairman, but even that couldn't have made the Bureau much happier. This was direct access to information in black and white so badly needed, to letters and rosters and directives. This was direct access to potential proofs that might be undeniable in courts of law or before Congressional hearings.

When I told Ed White about it, he forgot himself almost to the point of raising his voice. As for me, I came down with interior butterflies and loss of appetite. But I went to work, right up to my neck this time, for the Communist Party of the United States of America.

To this day an ultimate evaluation of my findings in that critical post plus all my other findings as a counterspy is not possible. The majestic honor of democratic justice has also a majestic slowness. Appeals may be made indefinitely and always there is the word pending. Pending, pending, pending. I have appeared three times before Governmental hearings and said what I must. The FBI has an avalanche of my reports, some apparently meaningless in themselves but of significance to the Bureau as it fits piece on piece into its giant, never-ending jigsaw puzzle. But even the most astonishing turns of good fortune, yielding windfalls of material evidence, assume a modest perspective when the fundamental honor of our law sets in motion its ponderous digestive system.

One day quite early in my Communist career, we got a break of staggering proportions—plus a scare that would have robbed anyone but my agile husband of ten years of his life. Following a few scattered raids in the East and Middle West of various Communist headquarters, there was a report to us that the Los Angeles Committee for Protection of Foreign Born was next in line. Downtown there was panic, and I allowed myself a mildly bold step. I was reminded by a very high muckamuck indeed in local Red circles that my husband's garage studio might be a good place to hide the office records until the heat was off; had been determined already that hidden they must be. By phone, Paul enthusiastically supported the idea, and the records were moved to our place that night. The Bureau had been advised and was prepared.

As soon as the Reds had gone, the Bureau moved in, equipped with some of the most elaborate photographic paraphernalia I have ever seen. In their methods, moreover, there was a degree of perfectionism I had never conceived of until then. As each document and letter was photographed, it was replaced with the very wrinkles in the paper exactly where they had been to begin with. Each knot was retied as it had been tied in the first place. If a drawer were slightly open when it arrived, then it was slightly open when the Communists came back. But there was the haunting fear that the comrades suspected us, or would come storming back for something they must have while the Bureau men were still at work.

To forestall a possible catastrophe, Paul was stationed in the driveway while the Bureau worked behind a closed door. The danger was real, and more acute because Communists have the arrogance and manners of unbroken animals. As early as this they had pursued the habit of dropping in on us whenever and however they wished, never phoning and often pushing open the door without ringing the bell. Why not? Were we not all as one? It is not remarkable that even in the first months of my work, the first hints that Marion Miller consorted with Reds had begun to waft through the neighborhood.

And this night, sure enough—a comrade returned. His car pulled up not fifty yards from where the Bureau men had parked and he advanced toward Paul, carrying yet another packing case. Twenty yards further on, the Bureau men, alerted by Paul's intentionally loud greeting, stood flat against the wall, ready to leave the garage by a back door. Paul thinks fast on his feet, thank God, and was full of righteous indignation.

"You damn fool!" he said, before the comrade could open his mouth. "At a time like this, with every moment crucial, you come to my house! At a time like this, when none of us knows whether or not he's followed. With neighbors who look out windows! With a packing case in your hands! What do you want?"

He had judged his man correctly; this comrade was a sheep.

"Only to deliver this one more file," he said. "It was forgotten, comrade."

"Don't call me that, you goddam idiot! Give me the case and get out of here. Fast! I'll handle it."

"But listen . . ."

"Fast, fast, fast! And now!"

The sheep ran. But it was a careful half hour before the photographers got back to work.

Once in my pre-Communist days, had I thought of an incident like this, I would have thought, so what? Where would the danger have been? Where is your element of peril? In suburbia of these United States, would Communists or any other group of maladjusted crackpots resort to violence? Actually to *murder?*

We've thought about this a good deal. We've had to. I will tell you now what we have concluded and on this rest my case for the paralyzing frights I suffered and at last the ulcers from which I collapsed. In the daytime light of rationality, we cannot believe that a hard-core professional Communist would murder a political enemy, such as a Government spy, let alone a defector from the ranks—unless the provocation were unbearably extreme or he were ordered to do so by Moscow. As to this last, only the dead can testify. Not here in America he woudn't. I do not speak of moral compunctions, only the fact that it wouldn't be a smart thing to do. Career Communists are smart and they are realists, once we waive the fantastic nature of the premise on which all their actions are rooted.

But Communism has its own hulking share of neurotics and psycopaths, and these most positively will kill, and they have killed. You may call them a lunatic fringe, uncontrolled lunacy orbiting about a central deluded evil, and that's what it amounts to—but the bullet is just as fatal, the knife as sharp. So long as Communist discipline was maintained, Paul and I, if caught red-handed, risked nothing but a brutal beating, Paul at the hands of both men and women, I at the mercy of the women. He might have been hospitalized; I'm sure I would have lost every hair in my head. But now that the main damage has been done and I have publicly acknowledged my counterspy activities, the Red directorship may not wish to go beyond threats. That is comforting, but just to a very limited degree. We *have* been shot at, and whether or not the shot was ordered by top Communist policy does not alter the grim reality. We cannot stand guard over the children every minute of the day—Paul, Jr., and Betsy, for example, go to school on their own—and we can merely pray for the protection of crowds and daylight. Paul carries a pistol much of the time and keeps another always within quick reach. For years now I have succumbed to exhaustion much more easily than I should.

Has it all been worth it? I have to say yes. The price is right. It's been a high price, absolutely the retail mark-up, but still right. We can face ourselves and each other, day in, day out.

Yet I can remember other times when the price has seemed more than can be borne. I had been with the Party for three years and enjoyed its qualified confidence when I came across the young man I will call John. John was a cerebral Communist, a campus revolutionary from a good school who had been trapped by one of the intellectual convulsions that lie in wait for the nomadic thinker. God help us, but the young neurotics with the high IQ are superb material for the Communist psychology John had progressed fast from a certain daffiness over civil rights to the whole Communist challenge. He became fanatical.

Now it is not easy for a fanatic to fall in love but John had managed that, too—I imagine before he went overboard. The girl we can call Patricia; there is no point now in resurrecting real names from this terrible episode. Patricia was a wonderful girl and John did love her but she became intellectual anathema to him, to the wanton destructiveness of his convulsion. Her arguments for sanity inflamed him in the way a devout socialist would be inflamed by a move to canonize Barry Goldwater. He was an ardent member of a Communist club whose meetings I attended.

In time I met Patricia, but always in my habitual guise of an inflexible Communist. I'm both sorry and glad to say that she hated the ground I walked on. But there was something I could try to do, and I did try.

The first night I talked to her, while John was out getting beer, she said to me quietly: "I can't stand having you here. I want you to know it. I'm going to wash the walls when you go. All of you and what you believe make me want to vomit. I can only ask God to help John, but I'm not sure they're on speaking terms any more. My God is not an all-forgiving God. I think He has to carry grudges of His own. How can He love and forgive John when John disavows His existence. How I hate you all for what you're doing to John."

My acting was still in the amateur class but inevitably it had improved. To Patricia now I said coldly: "My dear, your feelings don't matter to us. As a matter of fact, these emotional outbursts are childish. Furthermore, I wouldn't save John for you if that were the point. But I do want to save the Party from him, so maybe you can stop worrying. If I have my way, we're going to get rid of this boy. A Communist who is not all Communist is no good to us, and as long as he loves you, he's a divided person. How do we know how much weight your word will have with him? He might hurt us badly. I'm thinking only of the

Party. I'm going to tell them this. But if you get him back, all of him, don't send me a thank-you note. You're not important."

The speech made me nervous. Patricia had been a Marine in World War II and may have learned judo from one of her gyrene friends. But she just went to the door, opened it, and said: "Get out now. You don't like beer anyway. You said so."

"Well, gladly. But what will you tell John?"

"Just what I've told you."

"May I suggest you don't?"

"You may suggest anything. Only go."

It's no fun to be hated, but here there was a little mitigation. To explain it, I have to make a cruel point but a true one. It reminded me of the time I broke an ankle and, after I was off crutches and cane, walked limpingly to favor it. Onlookers thought I was a cripple. But I didn't care about that because *I* knew it was only a broken ankle.

Similarly, I knew I was trying to help Patricia. At headquarters, I argued bitterly that John's "divided loyalty"—my phrase—made him too dangerous to the Party to tolerate. He would have to go. The higher-ups finally agreed. John was told of the decision, harshly and without reserve. I was present when he got the news.

He was like a crazy man. For all I know, he was a crazy man. "Wait here," he said. "Don't go away. I'll go to Patricia now. I'll break it off once and for all. She'll call you and tell you it's so. I wouldn't betray you for any damn woman who ever lived, or for anything else. Trust me for another hour. You'll see where my loyalty is."

When he had gone, I said to the leader of the punitive group: "It won't matter whether she calls or not. He'll still have the conflict. We can never trust him."

The leader said coldly: "Let us judge that, Marion. You've had your say."

Patricia never called. I do not know what happened to John and I don't think I ever want to know. I never saw him again.

For in the days just before, Patricia had been approached by Government people in an effort to solicit her testimony against John as a dangerous Communist. In an hour her own internal conflict had become by far the more deadly of the two. It is a sadness of love that one or the other usually loves the more. Patricia loved John as John did not love Patricia. John was— may a layman make a guess?—a bit schizo by now. Patricia had told the Government men what she so desperately hoped— that John's love for her would clear his mind of its fey addiction to the Communist narcotic. Already, she said (she lied bravely) he showed signs of coming out of it. The Government agreed that if he did so, it would surely alter circumstances, and especially if he would turn State's witness. When the men had gone, Patricia—all this was in a letter she left behind, which I have read—went to her knees and prayed to the God Whose mercy she did not wholly believe in.

I cannot and will not judge the will of God, and I must not be flip about it. Perhaps He was busy on another line. John came to her from Communist headquarters the night of his threatened dismissal. He told her of what had happened. At the end he began to cry; he wasn't as tough as he had thought. He told this to a person we both knew, who later told me.

She sat silent. There was nothing more to say.

"So," he finally said," it looks like we've had it. I can't let the Party down now. It would be like cutting out part of myself. I'd walk the earth like a ghost the rest of my life."

"But you can walk the earth without me?"

"You don't understand. You can't."

"No," she said. "I don't. I wish I could. Oh God, how I wish I could!"

"Pat."

"The door's that way," she said. "I don't hate you. I'm not mad at you. Always remember that. Sick John. But you'll be well some day, poor sick John. I love you. Goodbye."

John rode the elevator down from Patricia's eighth floor apartment. But it all wasn't quite over after all. Not quite. She was waiting for him down there on the sidewalk. She had beaten the elevator. She had jumped.

I lay with a compress across my forehead. No tears. No anything. It was evening. The lights were winking on along Esther Avenue, the men's cars were getting home and turning into the driveways. The little boy who once had fallen off the tricycle was bigger now and had a hula hoop. Was this manly? Well, sure. A lot of little boys had hula hoops. He was practicing on his lawn.

"He's not very good at it," I said to Paul. Even to my own ears, my voice had a dead sound. There was no timbre to it.

"Who's not very good at what?" In the darkening room, Paul's boyish face was gentle and years older than I had ever seen it.

"Sonny. He can't work his hula hoop yet."

Paul did not turn to the window. "It takes time," he said.

"Yes." There was no use trying to talk around it. "Is there anything in the afternoon papers?"

"Just that she jumped or fell and she's dead. You know what they always say—jumped or fell."

"She jumped. I failed her."

The lines of Paul's face firmed and he was youthful again.

"In a minute you'll say you killed her. Don't. Self-pity can be fatal."

"So can jumping out windows."

"Do you want to quit?"

"Yes, I want to quit. I want to crawl under the bed and stay there a while and then come out and teach Sonny about the hula hoop. And then come back and cook our dinners, and watch television and wake up tomorrow and know all over again that the world is Esther Avenue and nothing else. That's what I want to do."

"But you know it isn't. You know that too well now. And it never will be again. That's what we get to learn, people like you and me. It's—part of growing up. Some take one way, some another." His voice had become surprisingly sad; not really his voice at all. "I should tell you I'm sorry for everything. But I'm not going to. I think at the end of the tunnel maybe, the land is bright. Who said that? Winston Churchill?"

"Yes. He was quoting."

"You didn't kill her," Paul said. "You know what killed her. You know who killed her. Not John. For that poor son of a bitch I only feel sorry. He's got to go on living. That's his punishment."

"Will he go on with the Party?"

"I don't know."

"Are you hungry?"

"No."

"The kids are, though. Give me a hand up. I'm stuck here."

"Lie still. I'm going to take them out and give them a little systematic indigestion. Paul anyway. He's been wanting a Monte Cristo sandwich."

"All right," I said. "If you're so lazy, I'll stand up myself. We're going to eat here and we're going to eat now. And after that, I've got a meeting to go to. Go whistle for Paul, Junior, Paul Senior. Let's behave like heroes."

All I remember about the meeting that night is that it was not memorable. It was par for the course. It was miles from home, in a semi-slum in East Los Angeles, in someone's apartment. Someone with a first name but no last name. Most Communists I met in the routine order of duty were the same. Just first names. George. Frank. Sonya. Beatrice. This is Marion. The lost, pinched looks. The hoarse invective, the shrill invective. The hatreds, the wish to tear down. We are against, we are opposed to. But what are you *for?* We are for the common man, the proletariat, the right to strike and particularly the right to win strikes.

I am paraphrasing, of course. Never once in meeting did I raise a question except in the rare instances, like John when I thought I could help Patricia without bringing suspicion on myself. But they had a deadly sameness. No one ever laughed or even smiled, least of all myself.

But if I could have, I might have smiled at the continued determination to soft-pedal the word Communism. Try to imagine a Republican or Democratic convention abstaining from the words Republican or Democrat. Difficult, isn't it? But Communist meetings rarely speak of Communists. "Progressive" is the euphemism. It is a wondrous piece of meaningless deception. I cannot hear them without thinking of what a friend in the Bureau once said:

"Under our laws," he said, "proof must be absolute. That's good. It shouldn't be any other way. But among us here in this room, we know well enough that if it looks like a duck and walks like a duck and quacks like a duck, it probably is a duck. Common sense and the processes of law aren't always the best of friends."

So the meeting that night was, I suppose, another meeting. I was too dazed to know. I suppose I made my notes in the protection of the powder room or simply kept what I heard in mind and wrote it down as soon as I could get clear and park somewhere. Charlie was going to Mexico City next week. Hmm. The Bureau should know that. Abner would be out Thursday. We all were exhorted to join the pickets outside the cruel and oppressive X Fur Company and distribute our pamphlets and other literature to passers-by. The literature would be waiting for us at the picket location.

And the repetitions. Communists do not like to let a point rest. It must be beaten to a pulp. Thus it was seldom earlier than midnight before we broke up. Eight to a dozen of us. We never spoke of "cells," only clubs. The word "cell" is obsolete, primarily because it smells so strongly of Communist fish.

When we come out it is dark and grim and menacing, and I hurry to my car amid the imagined shadows of menacing slum-dwellers. Have I slipped in some way this night? Didn't Frank look at me strangely? Aren't those footsteps I hear behind me? Frank's? What will he do? Shielded from view by the bulk of the car, I tear my few notes to bits and sift them into the gutter. I can remember what I have to. And switch on the lights and turn the key and start the motor and get away. Lord, but I am tired! Half an hour to home? At this hour, twenty minutes might do it. And another two hours to make my report, on the little typewriter that practically turns its back to me after five minutes of hammering and has to be righted again, or threatens to fall off the table. Like the Bureau, I do not assess or evaluate. Absolutely no editorial comment. No more than Frank said this, Sonya said that, Abner's working on something in Washington, we are all urged to picket X Furs. We Progressives.

That's what it was like—most of the time. I assume that's

what it was like the night Patricia lay in the mortuary, beyond boredom, beyond fear; the night—what do you suppose John did that night? Years later I read the revelations of Mr. Boris Morros and found myself envying the glamor of his Viennese existence. Plain old East Los Angeles sounds so raunchy, so non-*gemutlich*.

In the books of intrigue I read, the deaths are, if not dashing, at any rate sinister. But now it is time for bed. Good night, Patricia. Sleep as well as you can.

5

Love and Marx

COMMUNISTS ARE INTENSELY AND HABITUALLY SUS-picious, both by nature and by necessity. So, for the same reasons, is their enemy, the Federal Bureau of Investigation. One night, I remember, I was inordinately late getting home from a CP meeting in a very forbidding part of town. Paul paced the living room until he could stand it no longer, then called the Bureau.

"This is Paul Miller," he said anxiously. "My wife is working for you against the Communists and she hasn't got home yet. Is there something you can do—?"

He didn't get much further. Next day Ed White hit the ceiling. In fact, he's still talking about it. Even within the FBI, it is deemed best not to chatter about curricular matters over a telephone. Paul, as far as the Bureau was concerned, had been gabbing like Gracie Allen.

The Communists check endlessly among themselves. They sniff and they fidget. The careful and rather silly muffling of last names is only part of their precautions. They set traps as well, sometimes clever, sometimes as clumsy as their heavy-handed semantics.

The first one set for me was somewhere in the middle, I guess. At the headquarters office where I served for a time as combination typist and recording secretary, there were some letters to get out one night after dinner. Yes, I would be glad to, glad to. I called home, had a bite to eat at a nearby restaurant, and came back to find my superior putting on her hat. On my desk there was a paper bag containing something. It hadn't been there when I left.

"I'm starved," said the woman—Nellie R., who was serving as administrative secretary. "I may be gone an hour. Now about this bag—someone will call for it. I don't know just when. It'll be a man and he'll identify himself by saying William Randoph Hearst sent him—then he'll laugh. His name is Max. Now here's the other important thing. *Don't* leave the bag alone before he comes. If you have to go to the little girls' room or anywhere else, take it with you. But not in view. Carry it in your purse. Got all that?"

"Surely. Shouldn't I put it in a drawer meanwhile?"

"No!" she said sharply. "Leave it where it is. It's your way of identifying yourself to Max—the bag has to be *on* the desk."

"All right."

"But remember what I said about leaving it there while you're gone. It's come from New York by courier. We've been waiting for it a long time."

I would certainly have examined the contents of that bag if Nellie hadn't tacked on the last two sentences. With those, she was working too hard. At first she'd been plausible; the bit about not leaving it unguarded wasn't bad. But the added information was gratuitous. I didn't know why the bait was being dangled; I was just sure it was bait.

She left and I typed, making as usual my fourth carbons for Bureau inspection. I always did this if left alone. At other times

I plain and simple copied correspondence from the files, stuff I had not typed. I had let myself be caught doing this immediately, explaining that as secretary I had to maintain my own records in my own way. It was a stupid gamble but I had counted on Nellie and the others not being able to credit a deception this bald and deciding I must be trustworthy if weakminded. I thought it had worked, and I still think it did. If they planted phony documents on me, I never heard of it.

Nellie was gone for nearly two hours. All that time the bag sat there, practically throwing off sparks. On at least four occasions I was tempted to reach for it. But each time I remembered that superfluous lick about New York and the courier and the anxious wait, and held my hand back.

I finished my work just as Nellie reentered. The bag hadn't been moved an iota. She looked at it before she looked at me. I recall that *now;* I didn't notice it so much then. I confess to being a Monday morning quarterback.

"Done?" she asked.

"Just this minute."

"I take it Max hasn't been here."

"Nobody at all."

Max, or somebody who called himself Max, came in a few minutes later. Subtle timing, I perceive now; adroit as an ox in a lily pond. "Hearst sent me," he said, and laughed. He was a tight-faced little man and I'm not sure he had ever laughed before. In any event, he produced a truly horrible noise.

"Hearst who?" said Nellie.

"William Randolph," he said. "That the package?"

"That's it," she said. "Carry it in your pocket."

"So long," said Max.

Many weeks later, a Communist functionary with whom Paul and I had become rather close, since he was the man who gave us the necessary instructions and indoctrination before we became Party members, met us in my office by appointment one evening. Paul had been downtown on other business and he and I planned to have dinner together. There was work to do but I was being temporarily replaced by a motherly looking woman who came bewilderedly to many meetings. She did not have the faintest idea what Communism was all about or the slightest conception of its danger. She only knew that her son was out of work and her grandchildren were existing on skimmed milk and baked dough. She was ready for anything that would promise them more, and the Party can promise like nothing human. I told her what to do, and Paul and I and our Red instructor—let's call him Morris—went outside.

"Before you go to eat," Morris said suddenly, "come with me. I'll show you something."

He led us upstairs two flights to an office across the way. There he opened a door to an office bearing a legend I recognized as an organization affiliated to the Foreign Born committee, and motioned toward the window. "Don't turn on the light," he said.

In a moment it became obvious why. The office overlooked my own desk. The motherly woman sat there, typing laboriously. We had been watching for only a minute, puzzled and impatient, when Nellie came into view. She carried what was either the same paper bag or one exactly like it. She laid it down on the desk, where it had lain the night I had it for company, and we saw the pantomime of interchange. Then Nellie left.

The rest was predictable; classic, in an unpleasant way. The poor woman held out for less than five minutes before she sneaked a hand toward the bag and plunged it in. She withdrew some papers. Morris drew one of the loudest breaths I have ever heard, then exhaled it again. He said nothing. I had the crazy notion I would now be seized by him and pushed out, and down to eternity.

I felt I had to speak but could not commit myself in any direction. I said: "This is pretty dull watching"—as non-significant an observation as I could think of.

"Not as dull as you'd suppose," he said. "Remember the night that bag sat there with you?"

"No, I—Yes, I do, too. From New York. Someone came to pick it up."

"I see I haven't instructed you too well," he said. "You still talk too much. But let it go this time. Yes, that's the night. I was here then, too. You didn't touch the bag. If you had, I wouldn't be showing you this. Does it teach you anything?"

"Not—especially."

"It should. It's a lesson in minding your own business. In that bag are old grocery receipts and stubs from Santa Anita. This gives us the answer to what makes with Roberta." That was the name I'll give the motherly lady.

Paul frowned a little. I could see him in the dim light from the window. "Comrade," he said shortly, "don't you make allowances for natural curiosity?"

"We make allowances for nothing. Making allowances is too expensive. We can always get along without the Robertas."

"You don't think she's a spy, do you?"

"Thinking is too expensive, too. Now go eat your dinner. I'll see you another time."

I never saw Roberta again. I did hear that the windows in her little frame house had been broken by stones one night a bit later, presumably in lieu of a crack across the hand with a ruler. And they took away her nice, nourishing promises. But they did leave her something: the hope that pie crust and skimmed milk are nutritious.

Somewhere, somewhere, there is a young man—he must be twenty-four now—who may still be convinced I am a black-hearted bitch. This more or less was his terminology for me the last time I saw him. I wish he didn't think this but at the time it was imperative that he did. A secret-agent cannot change cloaks for convenience' sake or in the interests of good will. When you assume the role of villain, you play it until death or some happier circumstance do you part.

The young man's name is Joey. When I met him, he was seventeen. Seventeen and a Communist. It sounds absurd because it is absurd, but the Communists have an abiding faith in the malleability of the young. (I will tell shortly, how they tried to infiltrate a nursery—the one my child attended.) And Joey was young, all right.

There is a brief case history indicated here. Joey's father was killed in the collapse of a mine. The evidence was that the mine was a pretty slipshow operation, one of John L. Lewis' over-sights. Under the guidance of an uncle, his father's brother, Joey grew into adolescence learning gradually to hate mine-owners as a class. From there it wasn't much of a jump to hate employers as a class and finally all of that heterogeneous group he decided were "capitalists." The uncle had Communist sympathies and by the time he had exposed Joey to a few of the comrades, Joey was a pushover. The only indoctrination he needed were the words, "Come in."

But there was one hitch so far as the comrades were concerned. Joey's mother, despite the tragic loss of her husband, was bitterly anti-Red. She was an intelligent woman, who was aware of all the implications of the death struggle and of the infinite promise of the free world.

She was aware, but she couldn't get through to Joey. His bitterness was a thing of the heart and the viscera, and Communists are adept at inflaming both. Joey didn't know a collective from a collection agency, but he knew that all capitalists were bastards and all Communists, by mathematical reverse logic, saviors.

Nevertheless, he became a serious problem to the Party— or more accurately, his mother did. They regarded her possible influence on him as baleful—and she regarded theirs as equally so. She forbade the use of her home as a Communist meeting place; she intercepted Joey's mail; and she destroyed the literature he brought home for distribution. The Communists did what they could to offset her but despite them, she was making some progress. It wasn't much but it was enough to bring Joey before a Communist review board. Our Red comrades like to keel-haul defectors before they have a chance to defect.

I was part of that review board. I had been a "loyal Communist" for years now and was allowed to take part in disciplinary action. Some of the time I didn't mind, but for cold-blooded reasons. In the case of Joey, my reasons were more complex. For one thing, he was just a kid and basically a nice kid. For another, I wanted to do his mother a favor. For a third, the case was in many respects a counterpart of my doomed, abortive effort to help John and Patricia.

Joey came before the board looking somewhat beat up. He had been. Our goons had tried to slap some reason into him— foolish, but goons always are.

One of the comrades took the lead, in words Joey could not possibly have comprehended. It was a woman. "Mother love," she said, "is a contemptible thing, a bourgeois thing. Just as logically, love for mother is contemptible. It is soft and gicky, like mush and mud, and it will betray you, and when it does, you will betray us. That isn't all. When you betray us, you have betrayed what your father died for (a wild misstatement of fact; his father had died most unwillingly and not for a cause) and what every worker is willing to die for, and many must. You will be a traitor to your class and to the eternal battle for justice and the human race. Face what you must now, tonight: abandon us, the army that is the hope of the world, or abandon this silly woman whom through biological accident you call your mother. I do not mean intentionally to insult your mother. She can't help being silly or a biological accident. But that does not excuse your letting her stand in the way of your only mission in life. Of the only mission there is in life for the en-lightened. Think about it but don't think too long."

She had thrown up just the right amount of coherent fire-works to confuse Joey and kindle his volatile emotional fuel. He pulled himself straight. "I am a Communist, comrade," he began. "I'm a Communist before I'm a son, if that's what you're getting at. I'm a Communist before I'm anything, and I'll go to mother and tell her—"

I have said that my abilities as an amateur actress were look-ing up, largely because they had to or else. I rose now and interrupted Joey.

"Shut up," I said to him. Then, to the review board: "Why do you listen to this kid? In the language of the capitalist gut-ters, he's a punk. He's also a mama's boy, no matter what he says here, and there's no worse risk in the world than a mama's boy unless it's someone in love with a bourgeois. The Party's in delicate straits now. We can't afford risks. What if he does stay with us? If he doesn't run to the authorities, his mother will. Aren't there enough investigations without our getting sentimental over a—punk. I've never used that word before but I'm using it now. You pride yourselves on being realists. We all do. Well, let's *be* realists and stop crying over one youngster. Don't give the choice to him. I say we should take the initiative. Throw him out. Let's say 'Get out' to Joey before this meeting is over."

Somewhere in that sprawling diatribe, I must have hit the proper note. A crestfallen Joey was, so to speak, excommunicated. There was no further punishment—unless it was to me.

Months later, I bumped into Joey and his mother coming out of a super market. Joey saw me and turned white.

"You're the Miller bitch," he said.

"Joey!" His mother turned to me, stricken, by his language, I believe, more than anything else.

"Let me finish," he said. "I don't thank you for a thing and I never will, but I'm glad you got them to throw me out of that rotten bunch of Russkies you go with. You don't know what I've learned since then and the people I've met, and now I understand a lot of things. Like I understand you. You'll never know the favor you did me. I must have been nuts. But anyway I had an excuse. I was what you said I am—a punk. What excuse have *you* got?"

"Joey!" said his mother again.

"Don't Joey me, mama. I don't owe her a thing, not a thing. She wasn't doing me a kindness, she was doing it for those lice she hangs around with. *Hangs around with?* She's a louse herself. She's one of them. Just the same. Thanks, but no thanks. You know what I am, *Mrs.* Miller? You know what I am, all of a sudden? I'm an American. That speech of yours didn't turn the trick, but it started it. God knows, you didn't mean it that way. So thanks for nothing. I hate your guts." He walked away.

His mother hung back for a minute. I leaned against the store window, deathly afraid I would faint.

"I'm going to be honest, Mrs. Miller," she said. "I don't hate you. I try not to hate. But I despise you. Not personally. Yes— personally. I'm sorry but that's so. I despise all of you per- sonally. With me it's more than an abstract conception. But I apologize for Joey and I'm glad you did what you did. I can't be grateful any more than he can but I'm glad it happened. It was a blessed accident."

I almost broke my covenant with God and right. I wanted so much to say, "It was not an accident." But I just kept leaning against the window until she walked off. Can you sleep more easily now, Patricia? A little more easily?

In the Communist war, there are mothers and mothers. I am one. Mrs. Khrushchev is one. And more and more and more. No one is untouched. You throw a stone in the water and the ripples spread out and out. Who among us is an island? Not a single soul, not a Ubangi, not a hermit who lives in a tree. I have not learned so much, though later I will say what I believe. But I have learned that. If you are not up front, where Paul and I placed our- selves, then you are nonetheless in the rear area whether you know it or not. Your life is touched every day by the crazed in- tensity of these dedicated zealots who tear at what they do not want, and know, even in their psychosis, what they do want. Yes, they do know. I will tell you about that in a later part.

For now, let's carry on with love, maternal division.

6

Mother Dear!

WHEN BETSY WAS FOUR YEARS OLD, I ENTERED HER in a nursery school around the corner from where we live. It was a pleasant school run by pleasant people in a pleasant atmosphere. I grew to know and know pretty well everyone concerned with it and could detect no friction, administrative or in the relations of teachers to pupils, save in the instance of one woman who seemed to be lecturing the children on subjects not connected with putting round pegs in round holes.

When finally one tot sternly informed his parents after school that their gardener should have ownership of their garden, since it was he who grew the flowers, trouble erupted, and culminated with the teacher being dismissed. She had also informed this thoughtful child that his father, the assistant manager of a drug store, not only was exploiting the clerks shamefully but was himself being exploited by the ownership echelon. The woman was a Communist, not of my acquaintance as such, who had been placed in the school through the efforts of a Communist-dominated employment agency. A week after her dismissal, pickets appeared outside the school. They represented a maintenance union. The school was being cruel to the teachers.

It was all something of a fiasco. Even the teachers refused to strike. They did not seem aware they were being exploited. The head of the union local was not a Communist, did not approve of the maneuver, and did not understand the orders he had received from his state superiors. This became clear at indignation meetings at which parents appeared in unanimous droves. Half the fathers were good union men themselves but could make no sense of *this* move. I attended some of the meetings but took no vocal stand either way; a state of rebellion against *all* my masters was fermenting within me. Many of the mothers shunned me. The "knowledge" that I had Communist sympathies had by this time gained considerable momentum. It was still agreed at Communist headquarters, on the other hand, that formally I was to acknowledge no Communist connections and, if necessary, disavow them. My deceptions were growing very complicated.

Some of the meetings were declared open and the Communists, of course, were able to move their members into these as representatives of the union. The Communist spokesmen demanded that the picket line not be crossed. They were for the most part ignored. One of the mothers who ignored them was Marion Miller. It was a risky and possibly ill-advised move, but I was not going to deprive Betsy of this fine nursery over what seemed no more than the possibility of a slight retribution from Party members.

The showdown so far as I was concerned did not come for several weeks. The pickets were pulled out very shortly. The Communists can and do support causes that are widely unpopular but not one where the returns cannot conceivably justify the investment. They were and they are passionately eager to get a foothold in the plants of American education, and on certain high levels they have a beauty. But even nursery schools are not beneath their attention. They had gone to some pains to get their teacher in there and they were willing to make an issue over her firing. But when their little uprising attracted the casual attention of a vigilant newspaper, they backed away.

I wasn't done, though. I had crossed that picket line, toting my capitalistic daughter behind me, and a month later the nominal head of the Los Angeles Committee for Protection of Foreign Born, summoned me into the Presence.

"It has come to my attention," she said portentously, "that you have violated a picket line made up of workingmen. Didn't you know this was instigated by Progressives? By our friends?"

"I guessed that it was." I knew what direction I had to take.

She turned a little white. "In all seriousness," she said, "how dared you? I can see to it that no Progressive organization in this town ever again lets you in its doors. How *dared* you?"

I said: "I thought it was agreed that I could be most effective if my—affiliation weren't known to my neighbors. What do you think they would have said and thought if I'd refused to cross the line?"

I had fallen back on the same shaft of logic several times. But now it didn't work.

"It makes no difference," she snapped. "This was effrontery. By crossing the line you weakened the movement. *Nothing* must weaken the movement. Keeping quiet, avoiding suspicion that way, that's one thing. This is another. I think you'll have to leave us. I'm going to recommend it."

I was frightened now—of all my work being canceled out, of Bureau disappointment, and, frankly, of the Communists. In snap panic, I made a lunge at her better nature, if any. She was, I knew, a mother herself.

"All right, I'm sorry. I hadn't realized."

She slapped her desk with the flat of her hand. "I can remember when you didn't talk like that. What's happening to you, Marion? You're not becoming a humanist, by any chance? What kind of pap *is* this?"

Even in my fear I realized I was confronted by someone fighting an awful schism, one many Communists must fight at one time or another. The Cause had to rise again and beat down the Mother.

Her voice was too loud and too firm to be entirely convincing. "Let me tell you something about my own little girl," she said. "She was four and this was in New York. We were walking. On Broadway. There was a sandwich man on the walk in front of a cafeteria. You know, they carry these advertisements on their shoulders. I took my daughter by the hand and started to walk into the cafeteria for lunch. She held back. She said to me, 'Mother! You're not going to walk by the picket! Shame on you!' " She sat back. Triumphant.

I didn't know whether to believe the story or not. I rather hoped it wasn't true. If bright sayings of children have to be pinned on little girls of four, it is better if no ideology is attached to them. Somehow you lose your laugh that way.

My hesitation may have shown in my face. She pressed on with another story of ideological faith versus mother love. The roles of parent and child were reversed but essentially it was the same story. Ideology won again. A man in downtown Los Angeles had been doing well with a small manufacturing concern, mattresses. His mother, an impassioned Communist, helped him in the office. In return he supported her. But one day when business was reaching its crest, a Red organizer was moved into the shop, unionized it for his Communist bosses and made demands on the owner that inevitably would have driven him into bankruptcy. When arbitration, which he readily agreed to, failed, the shop was struck. The leader of the pickets? Mama.

As she told the story, the dear old soul drove her son into bankruptcy anyway, since his business had to function or perish, and at the same time invited poverty herself. The Party was very proud of her.

But as she talked, I could think of nothing but an old and slightly brutal joke about a hard-headed Broadway character who had a million dollars and whose mother yet sold newspapers from a corner stand every night of the year, hot or cold, standing wearily for hour on hour until her ancient feet were hobbled beyond repair.

"But this is terrible!" someone said, on hearing of the situation. "Sam has a million dollars and the old lady is dying! His own mother! Why does he let her do it?"

Sam's partner overheard him and stepped in angrily. "It's business, you stupe!" he said. "I guess you didn't know—he rents her the stand!"

By the time she finished, my mind had wandered and I was giggling hysterically and unhappily, and I couldn't stop. I was sure she would call down the bolts of Stalin's lightning and strike me dead. But instead she became icily impassive.

"You're tired, Marion," she said. "And when you're tired, you're silly—go home. And just remember—don't cross our picket lines again. Not for any reason."

It could not go on forever, my fantastic way of life, with each compartment neat unto itself, no overlapping, no intrusions. A few days after his seventh birthday, Paul, Jr., came home dragging his feet slowly as though he wore snowshoes. His head was down and dried tears streaked his face. He had a split lip but he told me later I should see the other guy.

It wasn't easy to get him to talk but at last he did—of his own accord. He had been put to bed but he came back into the living room. Big Paul was working in his studio.

"Mother." Young Paul's voice was lifeless, hardly audible.

I had started to tell him peremptorily to go back to bed before the inference of his misery reached me. I said, "Yes, dear?" and took him into my lap.

"Mother. Are you a spy?"

So it had come, as always it had to and there is nothing in this world you can postpone forever. Some day, some night, there is a deadline. In a way, there was no security risk involved. My Washington testimony was done and the world—that is, a small and special segment of the world—knew what I had been and what I was. But my son was a child and I did not want to go into any of this with him for years, in any event. The gradations of right and wrong are so infinitely complex, even to adults. And this was a child, my child. I had hoped none of it would touch him till the time was ripe. But "times" aren't always ripe. Times are when they come.

"Who—who told you I was a spy, dear?"

"Some kid. His name's Johnny. We had a fight."

"Johnny who?" Then I realized it didn't matter. "Paul, dear." Where were the words? *What* were the words?

"Yes?"

"Paul." God, give me something to say. "Paul—do you know what a spy is?"

"No. Yes—I think so. Johnny says it's somebody who tattle-tales and gets Americans put in jail."

"In—*jail.*"

[92]

"Yes. In Russian jails. By Russians. He says that's what you do. His mother and father told him that. They told him not to play with me any more. He says a lot of the other kids, their mothers told them the same thing."

His hair tickled my nose. I moved his head. "What else did he say?"

"That you were a . . . It's sort of a long word. Common something."

"Communist?"

"I think so. I think that was it."

Well, here went the shooting match. Or maybe it didn't. I put my hand under young Paul's chin and raised his eyes to mine. "Paul, if I tell you something, will you try very, very hard to understand? But you must never talk of it because that will just make things more confused than they are now. Do you promise?"

"Cross my heart? Hope to die?"

"Cross your heart, hope to die."

"All right."

"I'm a spy, yes. But I'm a spy for our side. For the Americans. Against the Comm . . . Against the Russians. Against the people who hate us. Do you understand?" How could he understand?

"I don't think I . . ."

"Paul. Darling. These people who don't want their children to play with you because of me—I love them. But they don't know it. And it has to be our secret that I do. Some day they'll know and you and Johnny will play together again. That's all I can tell you. But you must never tell them."

"But if you . . ."

"Paul, you're only a little boy. But you believe in Mother, don't you? And you *believe* Mother."

[93]

He rested his head on my shoulder in baffled silence.

"You do, don't you, Paul?"

"Yes, Mother." Dutiful. Lifeless.

"And you'll never tell what I said."

"No, Mother."

"And you have to go right back to bed so you'll be up early for your music lesson." He was studying piano, the instrument to which once I'd wanted to give my life.

"I don't care about a music lesson." There were tears again. "I hate the old piano."

"No, you don't. Go to bed, darling. And believe what Mother says, not what the others say."

"They're all liars."

"No. They're not liars. But they're wrong. It's not their fault. But you must believe Mother. Mother is telling you the truth."

Paul's sigh was deep and hopeless and uncomprehending, the sigh of a simple old man, I suppose, banished somehow to a barren Siberian steppe. But he went to bed without another word. He could not eat his breakfast next day and when the piano teacher came, he could not be found. He wandered off somewhere that Saturday.

After that and until the end of my strange odyssey, there were no more piano lessons. But he never again raised the subject with the other children or replied to their taunts—if there were any, and I suppose there were. Paul, Jr., I think, grew up before his time that night.

Now that I think back, there are two classic authors in whose work the word "love" never appears: Dr. Kinsey and Karl Marx. Either it was irrelevant to their material or they did not have the courage to take it on.

7

Too Close for Comfort

ON THIS POST-MIDNIGHT LATE IN 1954, I WAS DRIV-
ing home from Venice, a beach community south of West Los
Angeles, lately famous for beatniks but then just a community
named Venice that for some reason was a favorite gathering
place of Communists, and I understand still is. The meeting
that night had contained a lurid piece of information, an utter
lie as it turned out but one I could not be expected to recognize, and after I left I'd stopped at a diner whose owner I
knew well and sat in a back booth over coffee making detailed
notes from memory.

I am not going into the foolish nature of the thing at any
length, but the gist of it was that a featured speaker had told
the gathering that the Party would like to get a trusted in-
formant into the office of the FBI in Los Angeles. Possibly the
man was drunk. Communists I have known do not as a whole
drink much, but this man's boast was as foolish as his tongue
was indiscreet. If his contention had been true, the Communists
would have thrown him to piranha fish for speaking out in
public assemblage. Even as was, he was halted by the leader
before he was through and ushered out of the hall in strange
haste. Nevertheless, his words had been uttered.

I had never got over my fear of retribution descending on me some time in darkness but years of uneventful evenings had distracted my anxiety some. Now I made four or five pages of notes in a loose-leaf book I carried in my purse, paid for my coffee and left the diner. I tossed the purse on the floor in back of the car, as I sometimes did, and started homeward. It was about two o'clock.

There was almost no traffic, but two headlights did appear in my rear-view mirror—and stayed there. Within blocks my fears had all rushed back. The headlights were too close and too steadfast. Surely I'd been watched by someone outside the diner. Or inside? Had anyone else been in there? I'd been too busy with the notes to know.

Marion Miller, icy-nerved girl spy, went to pieces. Although reason should have told me I couldn't run away if my pursuers really wanted to stay with me, I accelerated. I did realize that to get at the purse and rid myself of the notes would have involved stopping the car and they would be on me in seconds, long before I could have taken the necessary action.

I got the car up to fifty, as fast as I dared drive if my life were at stake—as I was beginning to think it was. Stop signs ceased to exist. So did the more resolute finality of red lights. I ran through everything.

When another red light, a blinking one, went into operation over the headlights that tracked me—not even that brought me to my senses. There must have been some subconscious identification in my mind with Caryl Chessman, the bandit and rapist who robbed and molested women behind a false police blinker. I became rather addled with fear so that my teeth literally chattered. Believe it or not, this can happen.

I was still doing fifty when the car moved up beside me and the officer in the passenger's seat pointed to the curb. At the same time the squad car moved in just enough so I had no choice.

When I saw the two were truly police, I yelped with joy. They both got out and walked over. "Good evening, madame," said the first, in the courteous, ominous Southern California manner. "May I see your license?"

"Police officers," I said. "Thank God!"

That stopped the speaker dead for a moment. "Ma'am?"

"Better give her the drunk-o-meter," said the other.

"No, no," I said. "It's just that I thought— Well, I thought I was being followed. I was trying to get away. I didn't dream you were police."

"Didn't you see the red light?" said the first.

"Yes, but that scared me even more."

The second officer pushed back his cap. "Chessman's in San Q., lady," he said. "Now the license, please."

I got a ticket and a fine but I would still call it a happy ending to one of a number of close calls I have had, where I've been certain our Red brothers had me by the nape of the neck.

Incidentally, the Bureau reimbursed me for my traffic fine, which brings me to a brief digression. In their bitter attacks on me when my counter-espionage had been revealed, the Communists insisted I was a paid informer, that I had sold out their trust, that Paul and I had played Judas for money and nothing else.

This is an exceptionally clever lie. If we had done that, if this sort of gain had been our sole motive, we could never have washed away our deed. We were—I must forgive myself the word—patriots. We were compensated for our Party dues and other "incidentals," which more often than not amounted to twenty-five per cent of Party members' take-home pay.

In fact, to return to the subject of occupational hazards, the night of Venice was not in reality a close call. It was no more than an ephemeral fright.

I was much closer to physical danger the night of a talk by an extremely high-ranking New York Communist whom the Bureau had wanted for years to tie to the Party with indisputable evidence. The man spoke from a typewritten script on the subject of germ warfare by United States forces in Korea. His point naturally was that we employed this strategy with wanton indiscrimination, and he labored the theme for over an hour. When he had finished he tossed his script aside and walked away from it.

It was left there on the rostrum in the tumult that followed and when I passed by later it was still there, unheeded. That might have meant nothing except for one thing: he had made marginal notes and interlinear corrections in his own hand. With no one, so far as I could see, paying any attention to me, I picked them up and—the rostrum was chest-high—put them in my purse. It wasn't a good place for them, should a search be made, but it would do for then. Later I managed to get to the powder room, which had a bolt on the inside, folded them double and stuffed them down my bra. I wore a high-necked jacket.

Now at this meeting there was a Communist, a Korean, whom I will call Emerald Yong. He has been charged with Communist activity, and I suspect his deportation is no more than a matter of time. But the laws of libel being what they are and Communists being so prone to utilize any democratic law available to them, notably the Fifth Amendment, I must insist we call him Emerald.

There is no character actor in pictures or TV who could quite portray Emerald Yong. The most villainous looking among them all seem a shade too benign. Emerald used to take weeks off my life simply by saying good evening. This time I was barely three steps clear of the ladies' room when he clasped my elbow from behind and said exactly that. I believe there is an official record for the standing high jump; but if there's an unofficial one, I hold it.

"Leaving so soon?" he said.

I said I was, that it was a long trip home. My voice shook, but not too much.

"Before you do," he said, "stop at a friend of mine's. It's on your way. I'll ride with you if I may."

It struck me as a very bad idea but as perhaps a worse one to refuse.

"I'll be happy to. Who is your friend?"

He named a Russian woman I'll call Fanya, who later would spend a few minutes at my house trying to brainwash Paul, Jr. I'll tell you about it before we finish. If a mien more sinister than Emerald's were possible, Fanya's was it. Charles Addams, the cartoonist, has drawn Fanya. He just doesn't know it.

Emerald led me over to her and Fanya repeated the invitation. The voices of both were cold and even and the smiles which usually accompany invitations were lacking. The hall was emptying by then and the three of us, with Fanya's husband, were about to go down the stairs when we heard sounds unmistakably ugly and violent below. Word of the meeting had gotten around amid veterans' groups and some of these had gathered outside the hall. We read next day that many of those present had served in Korea. We went to a window and looked down. A group of those who had waited were inviting the exiting comrades to take them on—sportingly enough, one at a time.

Emerald and Fanya thought the back way would be better, and so did I. "Lady" Communists, if such they were, were not being bothered, but in my equivocal position, I wanted no part of any of this.

That was really an evening.

Outside the back door and while we walked to the cars, Emerald lagged behind with Fanya and talked earnestly to her, in tones too low for me to catch. Emerald muttered steadily as we drove toward Fanya's. He said he was a South Korean but could not forgive his countrymen for attacking the helpless and unsuspecting agrarians in the north. Much worse, he could not forgive the U.S. for coming to the "aggressors'" support, and he could not excuse Truman and MacArthur for being born. It is the contention of the United States as I write that Emerald is a *North* Korean and hand in glove with Red China from the beginning. There was certainly reason to think so even then. The notes beneath my bra seemed to crackle whenever I moved and it's fair to say I was not happy.

We were barely inside Fanya's living room when she turned to me and said, "Marion, you're pale. What is it?"

I murmured about stuffy air and the bad temper of the waiting crowd.

"Come into the bedroom," she said. Feeling this was indeed the end and remembering again the picture of a dead informer Paul had described, I trailed behind her. There she said: "Take off your jacket and lie down. I'll make you a drink I save for special occasions." I thought crazily she must have borrowed her dialogue from Colonel Steranov. With my back to her, I pushed the notes as far down as they would go, took off the jacket and sprawled—on my stomach. Now the notes sounded like firecrackers. She gave me a long and dirty look—I realize today it was the only look she had—and went out. There was nothing I could do. The notes had to stay where they were. I was sure she and Emerald knew of them and that I was a cooked goose, and that cooked may have been the proper word at that. After a long time she came back with the drink. Hemlock and soda,

I thought. It was the color of water. I said a deep and silent goodbye to all and drank.

Nothing happened except that on that one concoction—*it was vodka, white creme de menthe and something else*—I became drunk as a hoot owl. It must have been hysterical relief, even though at best I have no tolerance for alcohol. My snickers and general conduct became so alarming that Fanya's husband finally drove me home in my car, taking a taxi cab. If the notes were missed, nobody ever said anything, and I hope the Justice Department has been able to make use of them.

But never again can I write off the fears of the mind as harmless ghosts that pass in the night. They can be real—they *are* real—and they can be well nigh intolerable.

The Communist I have called Morris—our tutor and would-be brainwasher—called one night to say he was bringing a comrade over to stay with us till morning. He didn't ask. Communists never ask. He *told* us. They were at the airport, he said, and would be at the house in half an hour.

Of course we called the Bureau immediately. Our man there was courteous but non-committal. It all seemed fairly routine. We moved Paul, Jr., out of his room, shuttled both children out of sight, and awaited the visit.

My first and overpowering impression of our "guest" was that he stank—physically, he stank. His body odor was overpowering. But that casual unpleasantness was forgotten the moment he raised his face from where he had buried it between the lapels of his topcoat.

Not only was he a notorious Communist, much photographed for the public prints, but he was potentially a fugitive. As celebrities go, this man was roughly in the Gerhard Eisler class,

and like Eisler marked for deportation. For all we knew at the
time, he was permitted by law to travel outside the jurisdiction
of New York, city or state. But the presumption in our minds
was strong that his destination from Los Angeles was Mexico,
where Communist sympathizers are a tough lot and frequently
with handsome political connections. To this day, I think it
inadvisable to mention his name. What kind of outrage we
might be compounding by harboring such a man for so much as
an hour was something to oppress us both heavily. But the
burden of guilt, if not of anxiety, was removed by Morris. Morris had no intention of leaving our site, not for a moment, and
Morris was likewise there to prevent outside communication.

As soon as "Gregor"—that wasn't his name but that's how he
was introduced—disappeared into the room we had made
ready for him, Morris stretched out in our easiest chair, extended his legs and loosened his tie. He smiled a little.

"It's so long since I've seen you both. Sit and talk to me."

Paul, a man of action who suffers terribly when necessary
action must necessarily be curtailed, twisted in his own chair,
and for an awful moment I thought he was going to look at his
watch. He didn't, but he spoke.

"I want to talk to you," he said to Morris. "But I'm being
a bad host. I notice Comrade Gregor is a chain smoker, and we
have no cigarettes. Neither of us uses them. Ask him his brand
and I will get some."

Morris lost his smile. "I'm sure he has plenty."

"I'm afraid not. His pack seemed almost empty."

Morris shrugged and I grew nervous. I knew how badly
Paul—and I, too—wanted to call the Bureau again, but it was not
going to be easy. It was in fact going to be impossible as a
measure of remedial action. Morris took care of that. Now it
seemed to me Paul might be tipping our hand, considering the

habitual suspiciousness of the Communist mind. But maybe not. Or Morris, if he did suspect, might be enjoying himself in a sadistic fashion of his own.

"If his pack is empty," he said, "think nothing of it. Comrade Gregor can go without cigarettes indefinitely if he has to. We are a well-disciplined lot, you know."

"Yes, but he doesn't have to. There's a store right around the . . ."

"Sit back, Comrade Paul. So much good will ill becomes you."

Paul laughed. "It's not good will. It's a thorough reading of Emily Post. Suppose I phone for a carton?"

"Now, Paul, you don't want to phone. You don't want to phone anybody for anything. You want to sit here and talk to me."

So the phone rang. The scripts of our more climactic scenes always have been in the hands of experts. Morris rose immediately. "I'll get it," he said. You know by now he was telling us, not asking.

We heard only his end. "Hello? No, it isn't. Paul and Marion are out for the evening. I'm a friend looking after the children. I beg your pardon? Oh, my name is Carl Shawitz. My wife and Marion are lodge sisters or whatever you would say. May I ask yours, and I will have them call you?" He wrote on the phone-side pad. "Thank you. May I give them a message? Just to call you. You're welcome. Goodbye."

"Larry Tomlinson," he said, coming back.

I said, "Oh, yes,"—never in my life having heard the name, and fighting for time.

"Very musical voice. He pronounced 'Paul' as though it were 'Pal'." Had Morris's gaze turned hard?

Merciful God. The Bureau man who next to Ed White

worked closest with us. But never did they confide their name
or business to baby sitters, alleged or actual. Divine Power
sides with the resourceful, too.

"That was Larry, all right. He says 'hal' for 'hall', too. And
'aaful' if a thing's awful enough."

"Strange," Morris said. "What kind of regional accent would
that be?"

"I think," said Paul, "from having Scandinavian parents. I'm
not sure. I know his name originally was something else. Comrade, I don't want to be rude but why do you answer our
phone?"

He smiled again. "Let's say I'm queer for answering phones.
Now talk to me." There were faint unpacking sounds behind
the bedroom door; nothing more.

Few directives can strike one so dumb as a directive to talk.
It strips the mind and tongue of every syllable. We sat silent
and inwardly frantic.

"I'll talk then." Morris was growing expansive in the warmth
and relaxation. Apparently he had lost interest in 'Larry Tomlinson'. "You are becoming good Communists, you two. In
time, it will be a wonderful thing to be a good Communist.
What can you think of more satisfactory than a tomorrow
where you will oppress your oppressor of today? Won't that be
splendid?"

"I've thought of it," I said.

"We talk about it," said Paul. "We talk about it a lot."

"I was reading the other day," said Morris, "some article.
What was it in? I've forgotten. Anyway. The point was that the
Party here in America propounds no threat because we are so
few. Isn't that a fine state of mind? A comrade might have
written it. I am even told that one did. It has a sedative effect
on those who read it, those *good* Americans. My God, how do

they know how few we are or how many? What a naïve conception."

"Did I hear you invoking God?" said Paul, smiling.

"Oh, yes. I often do. It's all in one's viewpoint. Many think of Him as old benign man with a white beard. I think of Him as a not so old man with a full mustache who sits in the Kremlin and redesigns the world for mankind. No heresy is intended. Let me go back to what I was saying. Suppose the popular view is correct, suppose we are few in number. What then? The capitalist world here has a saying that a good big man can always beat a good little man. It will stick in their throat some day. For *we* know it isn't true. A good little man can beat a good big man whenever he knows what nerve to apply pressure to and how that nerve can be reached. Psychology properly applied works miracles. The key grip in the right place. The bastard Nazis were children where psychology was concerned, even in wartime. Before that they seized an ideology that was not exportable—and then tried to export it. Hitler was an idiot. When he died, it was one of the three times I have wished for a hereafter, so he could spend eternity in hell. I am an atheist and a Communist so that *was* heresy. But I wished it."

"I wished it, too," I said. "I am a Jew. Paul is a Jew."

"I don't practice the religion," said Paul.

"But you are a Jew." Morris' crossed leg had begun to jiggle. "Just as I am. I practice no religion but I am a Jew. This is ethnic."

"Not in my opinion," said Paul. "And not in the opinion of anthropologists. But never mind. You say you practice no religion but you do practice Communism."

"So do we all," I said, faster than I'd meant to. Paul had been abraded intellectually and emotionally for a second. But Morris didn't notice.

"Yes, I practice Communism. Why do you suppose so many of us do?"

"Jews?"

"Yes."

"Because our scars are forever." Paul had shoved his convictions aside again. "A thousand, two thousand years of hatred and persecution. With each generation, the wounds open and bleed again. None but the Communists will save our people."

"Then why are so many Jews opposed to us?"

"They think their salvation lies in embracing a popular hatred. The hell with these. I say in all earnestness."

"You've learned your lessons well," said Morris. "So very well. And Marion, you say the hell with them too?"

"Yes. It's one of the rare times I use 'hell'."

"Excusable," said Morris.

The bedroom door opened softly and Gregor stood there. "Morris!" he snapped. "Ein glass wasser. Raus, raus!" He was still fully dressed. Morris "raus-ed", more swiftly than he had moved all evening. Bearing the water, Gregor closed the door. He had not looked at Paul or me.

"You recognize him?" Morris said to us.

"Of course." Paul thinks quickly when his anger is not roused. "We see papers."

"You must forget that you did," said Morris. "Not merely for our sake but you wouldn't want trouble with the—authorities. Accessory after the fact, or what have you?"

Paul shrugged. "After what fact?"

Very gently, Morris said: "Shut up, Paul."

I said: "That was a reasonable question. He wasn't prying. Morris, can I get you a drink?"

"Not tonight. You don't want one either. Nor Paul. Gregor? *Gregor!*"

The door opened a second time. "Keep down your loud voice. What *is* it?"

"Yes. May we make you a drink?"

"Good it would taste. But no." And gone, and more silence. The sound of strung up nerves whined thinly in my rabbit ears.

"Here is something else," said Morris, as though there had been no interruption.

"The psychology of these so-called democratic peoples here is barbarian. Barbaric? No difference. Barbaric is what they call us. And Mother Russia. But what do you think of this? A little girl is trapped in a deep well. A degenerate criminal escapes for a time the gas chamber. There is a vast interest. The sympathies of millions of people leap and throb, for the unfortunate child, for the monstrous man. Yet each is only one person. Now let a plane crash, killing forty, fifty, sixty people. Americans read the first paragraph uncaringly, gulp their toast and turn to Page Two to find which movie star has been caught in bed now with what call girl. Mass extermination simply does not interest the vassals of plutocracy. They can't encompass it, so many dead at once.

"So they let us do what we must, exterminate in thousands and millions the enemies of the people, and there is no great uprising. Stalin admitted the purge to Churchill at Yalta. Who cared? If we anger their tender sensibilities, it is for no more than an hour. We know that, and it is good to know. Who knows but what the day may come when counter-revolutionaries give us trouble? One of our fellow republics, Poland or Hungary, even Bulgaria. Blood may have to spill. But will America care, *really* care? You know better.

"All her sympathies will be for little girls who have fallen down wells. For cats caught in trees beyond reach of the highest ladder. For the youth with leukemia as he is rushed to Mayo Clinic. I tell you, this is arrested development on a national scale. They will be blind to the end—when it will be too late."

Morris yawned and stretched. "The right pressure on the right nerve under the right conditions. That is the battle in the psychological arena, not the big against the little. I could give you a hundred samples but I'm growing tired."

But he had the strength to give us one more. It was the case of the very famous, the almost legendary, American genius who was not so American that he ever sought citizenship, although he did take American money. Hollywood and his own marvelous if limited gift rewarded him fabulously, but he now lives abroad. I have been told by excellent sources that any effort of his to come back here would end at any rate in agonizing embarrassment, Ellis Island and a return trip. There is a matter of delinquent taxes in large amounts but even these America will waive if this unwelcome fellow will stay where he is.

Morris told us the story as he heard it. Morris is a liar and a cretin but here he was on ground he knew too well to be disbelieved out of hand. The actor was approached by the elite of the Communist psychological spearhead. Advance parties had found his flaw in preparation: he had been a hideously poor boy and was inordinately vain. He was flattered in terms that to nearly anyone else would have been a parody of flattery. 'Fulsome' is the proper word, if barely adequate. The man knew he was a genius but would begin to doubt it if not reassured every waking half hour. The Communists took up the task of reassuring him—in relays. No seedy hangers-on, no ill-smelling intellectuals, no premature beatniks, were selected for this task. These were Beverly Hills and film industry Communists, selected for their rightful place in the great man's social and professional circles. It was a frontal attack on a bastion highly vulnerable to begin with—the comedian's leanings had always been toward Lenin and the fuzzy notion that the world's goods should be redistributed.

But *not* the goods of Charles Spencer Chaplin—anyone who has not arrived at this name until now should apply for a refund. Mr. Chaplin, Morris said, was and is a penurious man who stiffed waiters—"stiffed," Morris said, is the trade epithet for no tip—underpaid his hirelings and drove fair and honest businessmen to breakdowns with his usurious hagglings. His treatment of young girls, Morris said, was infamous in every sense, and to learn whether or not he ever paid in full his renowned criminal lawyer in a case involving alleged seduction, Morris said, one had merely to ask the lawyer—ask him and then step out of the way.

In short, Morris said, even the Communists (the "even" is mine, not Morris's) detested Charlie Chaplin. But the use they had for him was far greater than their detestation. Moreover, he was a pet of Moscow's whose good will was appreciated all the way up to the Kremlin.

The crowning Communist achievement in the instance of Chaplin, however, was the comrades' success in prying him loose from great hunks of that money he set such store by. Within months they had him wrapped up so thoroughly that he was writing checks like a drunken deck hand advised on reaching shore that he has come into a legacy of millions.

Virtually as valuable was Chaplin's support of Communist causes.

We had heard some of the story, as most people have, but Morris imparted to it the fascination that always graces confidences that have the ring of first-hand.

Chaplin has denied he is a Communist. I am in no position to refute his denial. If your own eyes and ears refute it for you, then that is your business and I would not mix in it for anything. I tell you only what Morris told us that night.

The effort expended what vitamins he had left. He rose from the sofa, adjusted its cushions at one end, stripped off his tie and lay back. "I'm sleeping here. Don't disturb Gregor. Bring me an alarm clock. Don't answer the phone, I will. I sleep lightly."

"I still have work to do," said Paul. "Will that be all right?"

"Do you still have the phone extension out there in the studio?"

"Yes."

"Do your work tomorrow. Good night."

Early next morning, a car came for Gregor. He was sitting with Morris in the kitchen and had the look of having slept in his clothes. He still smelled like a goat. The drapes were drawn in the living room but we all heard the sound of the car stopping and the door slam. Then there were steps and a deep cough. Morris carried Gregor's suitcase as far as the front door. I saw fleetingly the man who had come but did not recognize him. Gregor and Morris murmured for a little while, then Gregor went away, without saying thank you or anything else. Morris came back to the kitchen and loosened his tie again.

"Shall we have breakfast?" he said.

Morris had a business of his own. The point is that no capitalist employer was demanding his presence that morning and he was in no hurry to go.

Gregor had left about seven. Morris stayed close by us until two, more than the time it would have taken a car to drive to the Mexican border at Tijuana. A little after two he left. He had answered the phone three times, identifying himself each time as the carpet cleaner. They were routine calls and he evoked no doubts among our friends and tradesmen. A little after two he left, having earlier made a small fuss over the children, who instinctively never had liked him. At the side door he waved to us cheerfully.

"I give you back your phone," he said.

I could feel my involuntary start. "What does that mean, comrade?"

"Well, you do like to answer your own phone, don't you? What else would it mean?"

"I see. I guess I'm not tracking too well this morning."

"You slept badly?"

"We're not used to strangers overnight."

"Surely I'm not a stranger."

"Not you. Gregor."

"Somebody else stayed here? You must have dreamed it. There was only me."

"That's right. I remember now. I dream all kinds of things."

"What a lovely pupil you are. You and Paul. Say hello to the children."

"Hello to the children," said Paul.

"Save your levity," said Morris, unsmiling. "You may need it some time." He was gone.

In the excitement of at-last, we paid no attention to his sign off. He had scarcely vanished in the direction of Westwood Boulevard when I picked up the phone. My Bureau contact of the day, when I got through to him, sounded jocular and rested. I stammered from excitement.

When I became unintelligible, he cut me off. "I know," he said. "You had overnight guests. Two, wasn't it?"

"You *knew?*"

"We knew, Marion, Your first call interested us too much not to follow up. Tell me, was it Morris who answered the phone? You remember Larry Tomlinson, I'm sure."

"I—I surely do. Yes, it was Morris. But all this time you knew and you didn't—you didn't . . . Oh, but we were dying to call you again! We almost gave ourselves away. Maybe we did."

He turned grave. "I hope not. The other one—what did he call himself."

"Nothing. He hardly spoke. Morris called him Gregor."

"Gregor, I see. And was he a satisfactory guest?"

"We saw him just four times. When he came in, twice in the evening, when he left."

"Do you happen to know if he bathed?"

I probably winced. "I do happen to know. He didn't."

There was a sound that was like laughter. "We noticed the same thing at the airport. All the perfumes of Araby plus a week's accumulation of good proletarian sweat. I'd rather not stand downwind from Gregor. Thanks for calling, Marion, and don't worry about a thing."

"But aren't you going to . . . ?"

"Sssshh. Yes, when we're ready, we're going to. Right now we're not ready. We like to know what Gregor does with his spare time. You did say Gregor, didn't you?"

"Yes, Gregor."

"My best to Paul."

"Do you want to talk to him?"

"In time. Not now. See you later."

"Goodbye."

It was my first and last occasion for misgivings regarding the FBI and its modus operandi. Wherever Gregor went—and I never did find out—he somehow was diverted back into the proper jurisdiction. He was duly and punctually deported and was busy in Budapest and East Berlin last time I read, possibly cutting up touches with Eisler and Klaus Fuchs. That was my nearest approach to the international climate of the great conspiracy.

Maybe they all smell like goats. This in its way is reassuring. If you don't hear them coming, your nose will tell you.

Weeks later I worked till midnight on a Wednesday at headquarters, transcribing a thick notebook, all in the handwriting of a woman who is not officially the top Los Angeles Communist but who, in my opinion, really is.

Proximity to a prize like this had me in a delirium of excitement—so much so that when my then superior told me to take the notebook home and finish the transcription there the next day, I put it down to an auditory delusion of mine due to fatigue.

"You mean the notebook?"

"Yes," said the woman, rather disinterestedly. "You must be awfully tired. I know I am. But for heaven's sake, don't let it out of your hands! Lock it in the trunk compartment going home, and if you're stopped for any reason by anyone, police included, see to it that it doesn't get to them. I don't care *how* you see to it, just so long as you do. We know you're resourceful. But of course, there's no danger. If there were, I wouldn't suggest you take it."

I worked on the transcription all that night. It was dawn when I finished. At least I had that to show when the payoff came.

And there was going to be a payoff. Because that notebook, the original in a top Communist's own writing and containing what had to be assets to the Big Jigsaw Puzzle the FBI put together day and night—this was going to the Bureau!

I could not and did not wait. At six o'clock or thereabouts, I had it stuffed in a manila envelope, stamped, addressed, an explanatory note attached and in the mail. Now all I had to do was explain so dreadful a loss to my superior.

I did what I could. It wasn't very ingenious but it was my modest best. I called her in the afternoon on a few hours' fitful sleep, did not disguise the sob in my voice, and told her the notebook was no more.

She didn't even ask how come. She said, "Jesus Christ!" she said, "Hold on!" and she switched me over to the redoubtable director, who was pretty adept at self-containment but was this time in a state of unbridled fury.

"This," she said with no preliminary, "had better be good. Talk and talk fast and stop that insane crying!"

"The baby. B . . Betsy. She tore it up. I could kill myself! What will I do? I—I have most of the pieces. I'll pick them up and paste them together. It shouldn't take me m-more than a week." If she had said yes to that, I honestly would have had reason to kill myself. Into each life some bluff must come but the circumstances should not be as close to imminent finality as this.

"Don't be a fool," she said, and for a mad instant I wanted to make kiss-kiss sounds over the phone. "What about the transcript? Did that charming daughter of yours tear that up, too?"

"No. No, I've got that."

"Get on down here. Fast." Kul-*lup*. Dead line.

Halfway downtown I became nauseous and barely got to a gas station in time. The director was waiting behind her desk, her hard-planed, ex-riveter's face implacable. She took the transcript, slammed it into a bottom drawer and locked it.

"Marion," she said then, "are you with us? Are you truly with us?"

I know I was pale and when I raised my hand to my forehead, it was slippery with perspiration. "What a question!"

"It's a very good question. Morris thinks you may be working for the FBI. Others have thought so in the past. Marion, as
God is my witness, if you are, if you *are*, I'll break your back
personally. Over my knee if I have to."

The room went out of focus, then slowly came back.

"Listen to me," I said, "I left the room for only a few
minutes. I was sure Betsy was too small to reach up on the
desk. But when I came back, she'd been tearing at the pages
with her little hands—you know children—and *scattered* the
pieces. Oh, what can I do?" I was crying in sheer fright. It
was the best thing I could have done.

Her voice was still inflexible but it was half an octave lower.
"I've said over the phone, blubbering is no solution. All right,
Betsy did it. I'm ready to believe you. But it was you who left
the room and let it stay behind with that—brat of yours, who
wouldn't know what she was doing. *That* was you. Now I
doubt that you're up to being a responsible Progressive. Morris
said you and your husband both were a lot too itchy the night
he brought you your guest and that you tried to put your nose
in things that didn't concern you and that Paul sounded practically deviationist—before he thought about it and changed
his tune. You've done some pretty fair work for us, Marion, but
the past means nothing. We've been checking on you now for
months and we're going to check a great deal more. Just hope
to *hell* your hands are clean."

At least she had diminished from hot to merely heated. There
was no other comfort.

"*Can* you forgive me, one more time," I pleaded. "I . . . I'm
stupid sometimes and childish, but I'm not what you're thinking. You're a mother too, you must have known how it could

happen." I dosed myself then with a reserve plasma of dignity —affronted dignity. "As for checking on me, please do. Check until your checking apparatus is numb. If anyone says or even hints that I'm a traitor to Progressive beliefs, I say now they're liars. You know my record."

She rested her head in her hand for a second. A Communist leader's life, crammed with decisions as that of any leader, cannot be easy. Would that it were difficult enough to make all of them give up. When she looked at me again, her face was approximately human.

"All right," she said. "Forget it for now. Go back to work. I hope for your sake you have nothing to worry about. Because I'm not going to tell you not to worry. That's entirely a matter for you and your conscience. I don't withdraw the word irresponsible. It will be in my report. The rest we'll hold in abeyance. Now get going."

I worked till eight and got home at quarter of nine. Paul had made dinner for the children. I was washing up before my own dinner when the pain went through me. It centered just above the solar plexus but spread out from there. It was real, shooting impartial agony. My hands shook and my legs grew weak and I clung to the washbowl for support. I was not to know it for quite some time to come but I had the start of the great-granddaddy of all duodenal ulcers.

Gregor, Morris, a handwritten notebook, the director—everything that had begun in the fall of 1950 and gone on since. Well, why not—we are all not more nor less than the sum of our moments. But these things and these people, I know now, were the beginning of the beginning of the end.

8

Money Money Money Money!

THE COMMUNIST PARTY OF THE UNITED STATES LIVES in a condition of furious, scrabbling famine as far as money goes—and it does not go far. There are major items of overhead—lawyers' fees, the support of Communist-led strikers, reasonably generous contributions to any and every cause that may be linked in some way to the master Communist plan. There are routine items—rentals, the modest salaries of the handful of professional Party workers, the cost of entertaining visiting bigwigs. There are minor items—e.g., the hospital bill of a comrade who has got lumps on his head for speaking too unkindly of the American brand of democracy in free assemblage.

The money is raised in various ways. Moscow, I understand, contributes a little more than half of the usual needs but I cannot prove this. (But it quacks like a duck, yes it does!) Monthly dues are exacted and woe betide the comrade who gets too much behind. These are modest enough individually, scaled in proportion to the member's salary, but that is only a small part of the story. The larger part is the ceaseless demand for "extras"—there is seldom a time an emergency is not in effect—and these are simply slapped on to the dues without regard for earning capacity.

The Party has a scattering of fat cats, angels with great personal wealth and, at a guess, neuroses of varying severity, out of whom the comrades can take enormous bites on special occasions. These are indispensable and should not be badgered but coddled and spoon-fed with the honey of coercion, so that when the bite is taken they will barely wince. I am told a whole leg can be snapped off this way and carted away before the victim knows it's gone.

My special interest, however, became the Money Tree.

The Money Tree is a dandy little Communist device. It has a prominent place at most Communist "social" functions, which invariably are money-raising functions, since the Communists actually have few social impulses in the capitalist understanding of the word.

Let us say that Morris has a birthday. Morris is not a very consequential functionary—his importance to Paul and me in this narrative is out of proportion to his mild importance in the Party—but he does have a birthday, which is a useful gadget. The comrades are prepared for this in advance and issued "invitations" by mail and phone. The gay event will take place at —well, Josephine's home—and there will be fun and games.

Fifty to a hundred may attend. Everyone yaks. The yakking is a babble and every bit of it centered on such fripperies as social justice and what a hell of a note the Rosenberg deal was.

Earl Browder, out of favor, suddenly is not just a political dissenter by a fellow who could be expected to eat his young, given any provocation, and the prosecution of Judith Coplon was a Fascist-inspired fabric of lies.

There is punch to drink, sandwiches which taste like dried bread and Kleenex, and an atmosphere of urgency that seems at odds with a function as ostensibly giddy as Morris's birthday.

And in a corner there stands a tree, utterly bare except for a ten-dollar bill affixed to the top like a star at Christmas. We capitalists know that hatcheck girls scatter a number of quarters and half-dollars on their trays as proof incontrovertible that everybody tips. Communists know that, too. The ten-dollar bill is a come-on.

Presently a spokesman bids the gathering "shaddap, please," and says that Morris, noble chap that he is, has decided he wants no gift for himself but would be pleased if in lieu of same members would attach donations to the money tree—for the Party.

This is no surprise to anyone and everyone knows furthermore that he or she is going to contribute. Each knows also that his or her "invitation" to the party is in fact an order and that Morris's birthday as such is no more a reason for festivity than a poke in the eye with a sharp stick. But the Communists like the motions.

It is expected that shills will rush the money tree first, taping bills (scotch tape is available) provided in advance by the Party treasury to the upper limbs, and these bills are more apt to be fives than ones. But sometimes the shills are trampled underfoot by the eager brotherhood, who figure and figure rightly that they are being observed by overseers with gimlet eyes.

The net take on a fairly successful evening should be between two hundred and fifty and three hundred dollars. Morris gets a two-buck fountain pen, a chorus of "Freeze a Jolly Good Fellow," and now and then an encore.

But if the take falls below expectations, say below two hundred, the comrades have other gimmicks in store. One is an impassioned speech in behalf of strikers in Arizona whose union is one of the very small number—and I do mean very small number—of labor unions in which the Party has secured domination. This speech may, in the interests of putting the affair on a playful basis, take the form of an auction—the speaker may auction off his hat, for instance—or a raffle for something of no value, or simply passing the basket. Get it up, comrade, if you don't mind.

And the comrades do, mind or not. The overseers have not relaxed their vigilance.

These collections, the tree and the auctions and the raffles, take place during the evening proper. There may likewise be an admission fee, by way of milking Morris's birthday for all the udder will give, and once in a while it costs one to get out of the joint.

But still the Party is famished. The state of economic malnutrition never eases. There are bazaars and there are fiestas, there are benefits, there are testimonials—oh, are there ever testimonials!

Some Party members, low-salaried to begin with, as the majority are, begin to miss meals that their master may be fed and fed and fed. The Party newspapers, from the *Daily Worker* (in my time) on down operate consistently at a loss and must be underwritten. Strikes invariably cost money, even should a retroactive settlement be negotiated. Lawyers—the Communists' lawyers are always thought to have Red leanings—send bills no matter whom their heart bleeds for.

Money, money, money, money!

In all these helter-skelter lunges for the capitalist dollar, I have seen only one geyser of exotica. (You may replace the x with an r if you like but it was not originally a typographical error.)

The wife of a zealous member, herself equally zealous and,

if not Lili St. Cyr, in any event the most attractive woman at the gathering, auctioned off a large share of the garments she was wearing. I have not before or since seen a strip tease with an ideological basis and a lawyer's fee riding on the garter belt nor am I sure I ever want to again. But it *was* different.

I do not think it was spontaneous, to put the thesis quietly. She had her own music in the form of records, her clothes all were equipped with zippers, which is not run of the mill in amateur circles, and her panties bore a hammer and sickle on the sitzplatz! But she had raised a hundred and forty-four dollars before she retired, still fairly decent.

Paul later called her the Jezebelle of the Ball, but that was unkind and unfair. She did what she did gracefully and in radiant good humor and there wasn't a thing offensive about her except her beliefs and her motives. It is not true that Communism as a sect is more libidinous than others, at least not in my observation. I would say neither more nor less. There are illicit loves and illicit matings, extra marital affairs, and so forth; but in fairness, no more than at a country club or a convention of self-made millionaires or, I judge, a given citadel of Wall Street. On one point only will I grant an exception. That hammer and sickle on the sitzplatz was something special.

Going home that night, I started to laugh about it and couldn't stop. Laughing I began to cough, much harder than I wanted to, and had to put my handkerchief to my mouth. When I took it away, there was blood on it.

PART TWO

9

Death Is Immaterial

LOOKING BACK ON MY FIVE YEARS WITH COMMU-
nism—five years minus one day, dating from my first Communist meeting to my first appearance in Washington before the
Subversive Activities Control Board—I find I have no ready
answer to the familiar question, "Didn't you think it would
never end?" I suppose I thought that sometimes, but only because I plain didn't know whether it would or wouldn't. In
terms of whether the years dragged or skipped, there is nothing crisp or final to say. Some of the fragments were tenuous
and transitory as a dream, others all but interminable.

There are meetings of which I have no recollection whatever, save that there was tedium and the driving back and
forth. They may have seemed long then, those evenings, but
now they are winks seen in retrospect. On the other hand, the
days following my father's death I can break down even now
into hours and minutes and they might as well have been a
decade.

Father died in the spring of 1953, of virus pneumonia in-
directly but directly as a result of a drug administered to correct it. That drug was one of those oops-sorry errors of medical
research and has since been withdrawn from the market.

His death came on a Saturday. The next day at home while funeral arrangements were being completed was not so much one of mourning as wretched loss and confusion. Friends and relatives stopped by our house, knowing as always in these cases that there is nothing to say, yet that they must speak.

The same confusion did not trouble Annette, a comrade under the Red banner. To my horror and stupefaction, she made an appearance with her husband. I knew her hardly at all. That I did not know her last name has no bearing on this, inasmuch as last names are not bandied about in the Party. But I had trouble thinking even of her first name. The house was crowded and it was incumbent on me to introduce Annette. Hurriedly in an undertone, I asked, "Annette what?"

She stiffened. "You know better than that, Marion."

"For heaven's sake, don't be silly. I can't just leave you two standing here. It'll look suspicious, later." Even *in extremis*, I was functioning.

"Make it Smith," she whispered back.

"*Is* it Smith?"

"Of course not."

"Then tell it to me. Someone may recognize you or remember. You know you can trust me."

So she told me. It was nearly as simple as Smith.

It was my first guileless impression that Annette had come to condole and I was a little warmed. No one else from the Party had appeared or called. I thought she might in fact bear the group condolences of other comrades. Bereft, one accepts comfort indiscriminately. The deepest antagonisms are for the moment set aside. Then again, my other master, the FBI, had readily granted me as much leave as I should wish without questioning my need for it.

But Annette had something else in mind; indeed, something

quite opposite. It was an "important" meeting set for the next night, the night before my father's funeral. She followed me to an unoccupied bedroom and made it plain.

"I've been told to instruct you," she said when we had closed the door, "that you must be there. We were afraid you might conk out on us." There were ramifications to the meeting's subject matter that only I, as recording secretary, had clearly in mind.

I should have been beyond shock by then but I was not. "Annette, you must be fooling. My father died yesterday. *Yesterday!* You can't expect . . ."

She said without inflection, "But we *do* expect. Do you want us to blubber like children? The meeting's critical, Marion. I don't have to tell you that."

"But my *father—*"

"Your father, your father, your *father!* What in the world kind of Progressive are you? Don't you know there's nothing in the world less important at this time than your father's death? Don't you know only fools let death stand in the way of the living?" She was growing angry. Then she saw me for, I think, the first time, and whatever expression of stunned incredulity I might have been wearing. She put an oddly leathery hand on my arm. "Look, I'm not being Mrs. Simon Legree. But surely you know your father doesn't give a hoot in hell whether you go to a meeting tomorrow night or sit here rocking your grief like a baby. If there's anything I detest it's this bourgeois masochism. The living are important and more than them, the Party is important, and the dead are dead. So much vegetable matter. Or maybe you *want* to grieve. Maybe it's important to you." There was a new edge to her voice.

What she had said about her non-feeling for death was true. I had reason to know. I had attended funerals for Commuists

where there was not a single flower, unless they were the re-
membrances of decadent capitalists. The reason was that the
Party demanded ahead of time of its members that they donate
instead the money they would have spent on floral pieces—
donate it not to the bereaved's family but to the Party. All very
practical if not wholly endearing.

I said nothing.

She persisted. "Do you like feeling bad? Do you look forward to feeling worse? Can't you wait to wallow in self-pity
for someone who feels no pain? No, not for 'someone'. For no
one. He no longer exists, you know."

Now for the first time I felt myself giving way to tears. I
had not cried before. Annette's dispassionate probe had shaken
loose what numb disbelief had held frozen until then. It was
true—he did no longer exist. He would not rise again to go to
the door for the paper, to look out on the ocean, the fog-laden
ocean of Pacific mornings, to think, "I'll call Marion," to say
to mother, "Think Marion's up yet?", to be hungry for his
scrambled eggs, to sip his coffee, to slip the sport section from
under the rest after he had read of Florida's newest hurricane,
saying "Well, we're out of *that*." I could pray to my God he was
happier now, but never again the sweet taste of the only thing
we know. Never—

"What time is the meeting?"

"Eight," said Annette. "Don't tell me you don't remember."

"He's *my* father."

"What?"

"I said, no, I didn't remember."

"Well. It can be excused. But you will be there?"

"Yes, I will. You've made everything very clear to me."

She patted my shoulder. "Now you're Marion again. I am

sorry, you know, about—all this. Anyway that's what I should say, isn't it?"

"Say what you like."

"But it doesn't matter. It doesn't matter at all. You'll come to see that. You must. Party members are brave about death because they know it's inconsequential."

"That doesn't sound like bravery to me."

"It is. Intellectual bravery." She slapped the palm of her hand with her gloves and started to draw them back on. "That's enough dialectic. I'm sure your friends out there would say there's a time and place for it."

I forced my mouth into an idiot's smile. "Yes, they would. They'd say the time is never and the place is hell."

She smiled too, not winningly. "They won't always say it. They may think it, but one of these fine days they won't say it."

"What do you suppose they'll say?"

"From their knees they'll say they always have been with us in their hearts but they didn't dare confess it. And they'll think we're believing every word. Now I hope I'll live till it's our turn. If I fear death, it's for that reason and nothing else—that I'll miss out on the victory we've had to eat so much dirt for."

At the door, I said, "Tell me one thing, Annette."

"If I can."

"Did Soso die bravely?" Soso is the commonest Red term for Stalin. It was a nickname.

"Don't you know he did?"

"I wasn't there."

"Neither was I. But how else would Soso have died?"

I wanted to match her callousness. I wanted to say, "Of shortage of breath, among other things, as we all die. Scared green if he had time to think of it." But of course I didn't.

I said instead, "Was Soso's death unimportant, too? Like the rest?"

She stared. "Why do you ask me that?" Annette, I believe, was stalling for time. Her dialectic had come a cropper.

"Because I wanted to know the proper thinking on that line. I have never asked."

She had her respite. "The proper thinking is that Soso's life was invaluable, his death inevitable. Marx and Lenin died, but not with an axe in their skull and not cowering in Mexico." It was hard for the Communists I knew to mention Trotsky's name. These days they don't know whether to talk of Stalin or not. Being a "good" Communist is an intricate business.

Insanely, the bizarre tension of these few minutes eating at my control, I said, "Did Soso swing the ax?"

Annette turned white. "This is nothing to you or to me. We work each in our own orbit. You're hysterical, Marion. Calm down before tomorrow night or someone will be asking questions." She opened the door and stepped out into the living room. "Where is that husband of mine?"

Mr. Annette, the only name by which I could think of him, was talking gravely to my mother. She gazed up at him, polite and uncomprehending. It would be weeks before Mother would care what anyone said to her. The face of all the years, the voice across the table, was gone. The years ahead remained, nothing more. Annette reclaimed her husband, drew him on as she had the gloves, and they were gone.

There was an aftermath. Annette's penetrating sense of economic values as they affected the Party were much more than idle talk. Months after my father's death, when Mother was living alone in the house they had shared, a Party member called on her and suggested baldly that she mortgage her home and lend the Party the money, repayable at one-half per cent more than bank interest.

At this date it is superfluous of me to say that the Communist Party carries a few seeds that may yet lead to its own destruction, and not the least of these is its crashing indelicacy. But here was a case in point; it may bring the observation home to you.

It was the Communists' idea, deliberately fostered, that Mother knew of my membership in the Party and approved in every way. The secret truth was that while she did not know the precise nature of my activity, she had at last been told that I was "engaged in important work for the Government." Telling her this much had been necessary. Both before and after Father's death she had been deeply depressed and painfully anxious over reports that I was a practicing Communist. One of my uncles, my mother's brother, thought I was, and a cousin still thinks so. The rumors had disturbed Mother so deeply as to aggravate her hypertension and thus labor her uncertain heart dangerously. The Bureau finally consented to ease her burden to the extent of a qualified reassurance. My own word would not have been sufficient. An FBI man told her.

As for the Communist practice of securing loans from mortgages, it sounded in principle like good business for the person approached, but was in fact thievery—"phony" is too polite and inaccurate a term for it. To my absolute knowledge, fully half these loans never were repaid, with the alleged "interest" so much academic nonsense. Party members who consented to such arrangements knew they were giving up the money anyway but sympathizers sometimes turned out to be a mite deficient in sympathy when it came to the Communists' welching on a fair debt. These the Party had to square.

Mother, when she was approached, was forearmed both by her quasi-knowledge of my work and her natural antipathy for the Red cause. At the same time, she was thoughtful enough to talk to me before saying anything unwise. She circumvented the issue eventually "on advice of lawyer" and on grounds that the amount of money she might raise was too small to benefit either her or the Party. Her reasoning was accepted.

Annette was not merely posturing that day at my house or talking for effect. I was to have further evidence of that creepy indifference of Communists to human suffering where it seemed to them extraneous to The Cause. Red followers call it whole-hearted dedication to an ideal. We reactionaries are more prone to thing it a brutality of the spirit.

One day in a Party office I was talking to a woman high in the Communist elite corps when her desk phone rang. From where I sat, I could hear the thin, frightened scream of a child on the other end. Since this woman was the same who had bragged to me of her tiny daughter's admonishing her not to cross a "picket line" consisting of a sandwich man, I had to conclude I was now hearing the outcry of the same little girl. She had been, her mother had said, four at the time of the sandwich man protest. That would have made her eight now.

On the phone her mother was brisk and imperative. I could hear the panic quality of the child's voice but not the words. When there was a pause, the mother said:

"Now listen to me. You are being silly. I'm *not* coming home now and I'm *not* coming home until my work is done. Do you know where the iodine is?"

A fresh, muted outcry, remote and unintelligible as a bad case of nasal congestion screaming from behind the thickest concrete wall in Buchenwald.

"Stop *crying!*" said mother. "I can't understand a word! I said, do you know where the iodine is? The little brown bottle in the medicine chest."

The voice was more subdued, its tenor halting.

"Yes. That's the one. Now. Put it on, put on the iodine, wherever the skin's broken. Do you understand?"

Very small noises.

"*Certainly* it will hurt! Pain is the price of happiness!" To a child, yet, parboiled semantics! "This is the lesson we've talked of so often." The woman's voice changed without softening. "Was it a big dog?"

A few syllables.

"Oh, that little mongrel! I know the one. You're too big a girl to be making all this fuss, hear me? Put on the iodine and don't call Mother again. Mother's busy." She slammed down the receiver. "You'd think my daughter was the first child ever bitten by a dog. I'm really surprised at her for calling. She's been disciplined *much* differently, I can assure you. Go on with your report."

I can only guess it was the mother's assumption that Communists are not subject to rabies, that only mortals have to worry about these. But this was after the visit of Annette, and I was under better control. I agreed briefly that the child was showing all the symptoms of bourgeois degeneracy. I finished my report, typed for another half hour, left the office and drove to see the child—I knew the home well. It had been the scene of several of those giddy "parties." If the child reported my action to her mother, I was prepared. I left a memo that was "important—am dropping it off on the way home."

The little girl's arm was badly lacerated but not, at this point anyway, infected. She was not crying any more and she was proud of her mother and herself for their respective behavior. The area where the dog's teeth had slashed her was tan with dried iodine.

"Did the iodine hurt?" I asked.

"Yes, it did." The child was solemn and full of complacency. "How'd you know I was bit?"

"I was in your mother's office when you called. Shouldn't we call a doctor?"

"Oh, don't be silly." Sometimes children mimicking adults are appealing. This one was just putting me in my place. Her lapse from discipline must have been momentary indeed. "Mother said pain is—is . . ."

"The price of happiness?"

"Yes. The price of happiness."

"And are you happy?"

"I guess so." She looked puzzled. "I got bit by a dog, didn't I?"

"Yes, you did."

She drew her small self up. "It isn't everybody's bitten by a dog."

"Hardly anybody," I said. "Won't you let me call a doctor?"

"Don't be silly," she said again. "You mustn't talk to me like a child."

Obviously I mustn't. I went away bewildered as to which of us was the child, which the adult. I felt a little as though pablum had dripped on my chin and I should wear a bib. I had been bitten by a dog when I was about this girl's age, a noble animal which, when I stroked it behind the ear, eyed me for seconds as if about to say "I love you," before growling deep in its throat and sinking its teeth into my leg. I had screamed in pain then, tapering off after the doctor's visit into sobs that lasted for half an hour. And now in my early thirties, I knew that if I were bitten by a dog again I would behave in approximately the same manner, give or take a few minutes and a little volume.

For just a little while, this Communist obeisance to stoicism gave me pause. Was another master race truly in the making? Were we capitalists, as some of our own politicos had warned us, growing flaccid beyond repair? Was there some stuff they were made of and we were not? Maybe. The stuff that won't call a doctor for one's own injured child, that hangs up the phone on its terrified cries and gets back to work without a break in stride. These may one day own the world—but not if I have anything to say about it. If another dog bites me, I thought that evening getting out of my car, I'm going to bite him back.

It was reassuring even if it was only a vagrant, foolish thought. Mother and daughter combined hadn't got around to mentioning that.

So if death is immaterial to the Communist drive and ultimate Communist objectives, then physical discomfort is even more so, if it is possible for one thing to be "more immaterial" than another. Let's say instead that death is not quite always immaterial—Stalin's, for example, triggered a holocaust—whereas discomfort invariably is. Insurgence in the ranks is so rare as to be worth noting.

My first observation of it took place in 1951 and led to a snide little piece of business on my part—which nevertheless I would do again. Two men among the Los Angeles Party faithful were ordered deported. (Now in 1960 they're still around.) The Party, fighting the order tooth and nail with every legal tactic available, thought it might be a good idea as well if a number of Party wives would picket the building of the Immigration Department, a line of march starring the wives of the two men. The wives' names were, we will say, Jane and Joan. I was also tapped.

Then the comrades had an even better idea. This was winter and the night set for the march was a cold one, whatever the Southern California Year-'Round Club may think of such a blasphemy. Hence would it not be an effective lick if Jane's and Joan's children, not far beyond the toddling stage, joined us —carrying, of course, their own little signs.

I don't know what these might have read—my horrified thought conceived something like " 'Oo 'Tan't Send My DaDa Away"—because the march never came off. Jane's youngest came down with flu, then the other one, and she refused adamantly to let them take part or to be away from home herself while they were ill.

There was rage in higher circles, rage and contempt and crashing directives ending in "or-else," but Jane held firm. A pretty sad Communist, Jane. She was a mother before she was a Red.

As it happened, she was not dismissed from the Party, but neither did she go unpunished. For a year Jane was banished to the canebrake—a series of sad little industrial towns in the central part of the state where Communists were seeking to pin business declines on business interests. While she was there, pressure was brought to bear on her husband to divorce her—he should not remain married to a political unreliable. But he managed to take evasive action; the beef was settled when she consented to make a crawling apology.

My bit of strategy, of which I am not especially ashamed, was to flounce into headquarters next day and upbraid Jane, Joan and anyone else I could think of for not going ahead with the protest. What if the children did suffer some—what was their health next to an effective public appeal? I was congratulated for not letting a few scattered germs distract my eye from the ball. Silently, I congratulated myself. Tricky Dick Miller, they were going to begin calling me after a couple more like that.

To no one in the least familiar with Communist internal policy will it come as a surprise that the top command urged Jane be divorced—in the beginning, ordered it. Party members accept such invasion of privacy as a matter of course where it concerns the efficacy of the whole operation. The Party has ordained divorces, marriages and common-law marriages—the man I have called Emerald and the woman named Fanya moved in with one another on orders. The Communist hierarchy has even redistributed marriage partners, and been unquestioningly obeyed, whether heartbreak was involved or not. To understand this, one must understand the spartan nature of Communism. It is not enough to mutter, "Crazy," shrug and turn away. Yield to so careless an acceptance enough times and you wake one day to find yourself in trouble—you and the rest of us. The worst trouble I can think of.

I do not intend to waste too many words here re-stating what has been stated many times by profounder intellects than mine. But it must always be remembered that (1) Communism *is* a religion, and (2) that nothing, *nothing,* is more important in the Communist mind than the end result. For this, any and all means are justified. Morality is not flouted for the sake of flouting morality—this, too, would be irrelevant and perhaps obstructionist—but it cannot stand in the way of political purpose. It just isn't important.

In the same way, you may yet be puzzled by why Jane, exiled to California's little Siberia, didn't say the hell with everybody and pull out. If you think she should have or would have —again you don't know Communists. Expulsion from the Party in most cases amounts to them to a death penalty, and resignation is unthinkable. Resignations occur only in the uncommon instances of intellectual revolt, and to one who is properly brainwashed, intellectual revolt is no easier to achieve than breaking away from heroin.

Yugoslavia's Tito, in the face of the most flagrant abuse from Moscow, never considered himself other than a Communist, nor did he consider picking up his marbles and going away mad. His nearest approach to heresy was believing in nationalist Communism over Russian Communism. Malenkov and Molotov did not flee into exile and denounce the creed that had kicked them so resoundingly in the seat of the pants. They would die before they would do it.

Avowed Communists, those who are committed both within themselves and by overt pledge, are not easy for us to understand. From my five years of really close association with them, I would take the stand that they fall under four loose categories. There are the lonely, who badly need a handhold on something, anything. Once involved, they cannot break away. If they should, they must wander off into space—psychologically impossible in any integrated society. There are the neurotics, in some instances psychopaths, whose viscera are full of spleen, their hearts simmering with frustration. They are not so much for Communism as for whatever is against an established order. It would not do to write them off; they are as dangerous as any, and in some respects more dangerous. There are the idealists, on the whole a fuzzy-minded lot, who are going to see a pink cloud if one points at a single object enough times and insists each time that it's a pink cloud. And there are the intellectually convinced—the ones nearest of all to a kind of stability. These are the leaders, the hard-core, the—if need be—utterly ruthless. To them the end justifies not merely the means; it justifies anything.

I would beware the word "intellectual" out of context. The intellectual Communist is not necessarily intelligent or the possessor of common sense. He has, in my opinion, arrived (at best) at the wrong conclusions from premises that originally might have been sound. He may, for instance, have started out with compassion. It is not ignoble to feel sympathy, even to feel pity, for the quarry worker gray with silicosis whose company-owned house is a dump. We dirty capitalists can feel sympathy for him, too. But he is a dwindling rarity in this country, and even if he were not, an authoritarian state is no more the answer than is collectivism. Your intellectual revolutionary honestly does not perceive this—though I detest giving him even that much due. He sees heads on pikes and a violent short-cut. Beyond this, it is not easy to say what he sees. Most of the massive thinkers in the movement I have talked to prefer not to think beyond the assumption of power.

I have, in fact, the impression that they would be lost and adrift once in power. Sooner or later they'd run out of people and practices to be mad at. What then?

I remember so well a vignette I read once—oddly, in a smart magazine that itself has been accused of Red sympathies. In the vignette, a Communist enters an Automat, encounters a mechanical failure of one of the dispensing units, and fails to get his two nickels back in the return slot. It is a Cause. Suddenly life takes on meaning. He has anger to embrace, direction at last where all day until then he had no direction.

Since he can offer no proof his nickels were not returned, the management brushes him off, whereupon he raises such a commotion that a policeman is summoned. The policeman listens wearily to both sides, then says to the management, "Gim'm his nickels, for Pete's sake. Fuhget it and gim'm his nickels." The management does—and the Communist is again simply a deflated, directionless, hollow little man. No more Cause, and what can he do with two nickels? His precious ally, anger, has abandoned him.

Some may consider the situation pathetic. But I multiply the little jerk by a few thousand and I'm afraid of him. I have no time to feel for pathos. Neither have you. This is serious.

One more thing I will say: the Communists would have dismissed him, too. He was useful to them only in the few minutes of his martyrdom. They have use for martyrs, as you know. They can and they do exploit martyrdom for all it is worth. The Rosenbergs were pretty sad sacks in the martyr role, and you hear of them no more, but even they served a purpose. Jane's husband and Joan's husband were handy as martyrs. The Hollywood writers who buttoned their lip and went to jail seemed vaguely admirable to the sort of non-Communists who are susceptible to Party coercion. I am coming to one of those.

I have been a rather involuntary martyr myself. Once during the height of my conspiratorial era, I fell in my house and cut my leg badly. Twelve stitches were needed to close the gash, and by a process of decadent bourgeois thinking, I called Party headquarters and said I couldn't make it to the office that day, explaining what had happened. It was foolish of me; I can only say I was in real pain and not thinking along proper proletarian lines. The woman I talked to naturally told me not to be a damn fool and get in there fast—what did a wounded knee have to do with my ability to work a typewriter.

I didn't work a typewriter that day, though. My limp was so pronounced that it drew some studious attention from top planners, one of whom presently called me over to her desk.

"Marion," she said," we're picketing the hospital still." They were—they were picketing one of Los Angeles' best-known hospitals and abjuring nurses not to enter! Evidently it did not concern them that sick and dying people were involved. "Get over there as fast as you can. They'll give you a sign."

"Picketing! But, my limp—"

"That's what I mean. Your limp. Make it look just as bad as you can. Hurry now."

So I am wrong. Physical disability is not always immaterial after all. Usually, but not always.

The Old Con

WHEN I WAS A YOUNGER WOMAN I THOUGHT THAT "con" meant convict, that a pitch was something a baseball player threw, and that a soft sell—if ever I gave any thought to so esoteric a term—was most likely a comfortable place in jail.

Today I know that a con is a practiced and skillful method of deceit, a pitch any kind of sales talk, and a soft sell a sophisticated approach to a sales prospect armored with a protective sophistication of his own.

Such a prospect for the Communist Party of Los Angeles was Carl, a young Negro, an honor graduate of one of the city's more prominent universities, and a brilliant figure among independent thinkers. The pitchman assigned by the Party to Carl was Ernest, the cream of the Communists' psychological cadre. I was the witness.

If it came to pass that a reader still entertaining an open mind on the subject of the Communist threat were permitted to read only one chapter of this book, I hope it would be this one. If at the end of it his mind is still open, then either I have committed a ghastly error of misplaced emphasis or Ernest is a better pitchman than I have dreamed. One of my purposes in writing this is to *close* minds against what is to me the clearest of perils, and I do not hesitate to admit it.

Bear in mind, if you will, that I have a grudging respect for Ernest. If I did not concede his talents, I would be a fool. The French, if I remember, amused themselves in 1940 speculating on the chances of the German *Wehrmacht* to turn the Maginot Line. One can hope their laughter stood them in good stead. It was years before they were able to laugh again—unless the Vichyites laughed.

Ernest was a highly successful lawyer, a Pole by birth whose parents had immigrated here when he was eight. He was *ex-officio* an "adviser" to the Los Angeles Committee for the Protection of Foreign Born. He had no link with them of record. Even less was he connected by record with the Communist Party. It was not simply that he carried no card. Ernest's peculiar status—which was not really peculiar by Communist rules —went far beyond that. He was not, so far as was known connected with the Party in any manner, not even by rumor or innuendo except in very special and informed circles. It was set up that way. So was Ernest.

In fact, Ernest himself was something very special indeed. He was one of a scattered few secret weapons the Party employed to assault difficult but desirable goals. He never attended Communist meetings, he never associated with Communists, his name never was mentioned save in privileged communication. By Party fiat he had the extraordinary prerogative of criticizing Communism should he consider this expedient to his objective. Nobody worried that in so doing Ernest might one day inadvertently convince himself that what he was saying was true. Ernest was diamond-hard of core. He was one of the intellectually convinced.

For recruiting purposes, Ernest wore the façade of his prosperity rather than the fevered dogmatism of the minority insurgent. He bore well the sheen of cynical practicality. His clothes were tailored flawlessly, he shaved his importunate beard twice a day and he smelled faintly and pleasantly of men's cologne. He was fortyish and good-looking in a way that wouldn't offend men. A sardonic cast to his speech made him particularly effective in the role of *anti*-anti-Communist. (Devout anti-Communists, of whom I am one, can be nearly as vulnerable to ridicule as Communists themselves unless they keep a careful eye on their judgments and semantics.) He rarely went over to affirmative Communism when making a pitch, and when he did, he was uncomfortable in the part. That was not because he believed less in what he was saying but because affirmation robbed him of his grace of manner. Professional critics with the sword of wit are at ease lambasting, not with the praise to which wit has no contribution.

Ernest had one of the upswept faces; all the lines were good-humored and firm and sure. It was the face of success, and his voice was mellow. Everything was as it should have been—for Ernest was a corporation lawyer! This always has struck me funny in a frightened sort of way—the true, undeviating Communist was a corporation lawyer. And one who went into his cases to win them, and did win them.

Is this an anomaly? It surely is—but not to the Communist mind, not to the mind that believes any means that attains its end is a pure and logical means.

So here was Ernest, and over there was Carl.

Carl we knew something about before we went up against him. I say "we"—I am going to identify myself with the Party for the purposes of this episode. Of course we always knew something about a prospect before we tackled him, but they were not often so promising as Carl. There evidently was just one serious hurdle—the thought of Communism in any form made him gag.

Sounds insurmountable, doesn't it? It isn't—not by a long way. Ask a Communist some time. Scratch a "liberal" and you have a prospect. And Carl, by liberalism's murky, maudlin, muddled lights, was one of them. Liberals I have known are incurable romantics who admirably think with their hearts and are apt not to have the faintest idea what they're talking about. You have to be with them, not against them, but the impulse to pour a pail of cold water over their heads for clarity's sake is generally a strong one.

That is the substance of my view of liberalism, and it happens as well to be the substance of the Communists' view. It's the only point on which we ever have seen eye to eye. This left only Carl the individual, whom we had yet to meet.

We knew he had many of the conventional liberal attributes, most of which he had expressed publicly. He was in pronounced sympathy with the screenwriters who had gone to prison rather than, as Carl said, "reveal their political beliefs." He delivered impassioned briefs for the Scottsboro boys, whose case he had read and re-read, briefs that alleged more than a miscarriage of justice. He was irrationally bitter over Sacco and Vanzetti. He was said to nurture an enraged belief that he had been denied a certain scholarship because of his race.

These things in themselves might not have raised the temperature of Communist recruitment circles, although the capture of Carl was ardently to be wished. What did excite our top brackets was a scouting report that Carl was an intellectual snob, the sort of poseur who wears cynicism like a cocked hat and revels in the stance of a maverick. Carl, the scout said, had no patience with majorities, solely on the ground that they were majorities, and was drawn to minorities for the same specious reason. His special delight was being a minority of one. This, I repeat, was our information, no more.

Carl was desirable to the Communists for several reasons. He was a Negro. He was clean, intelligent and fluent. He was well-groomed—how we needed that!—and handsome in the way so many West Indian Negroes are—thin-lipped, patrician nose, a fillip of British accent. He had a following of sorts. And it appeared he might be amenable to Party discipline. A superb potential front man.

Ernest was assigned to approach him from a limited takeoff point—membership in the Los Angeles Committee for Protection of Foreign Born. It had not been widely bruited about that this was being investigated for a Communist link. I was appointed to go with Ernest. It was not a compliment to my brain or persuasive faculties. I was window-dressing, as I had been before—not because I was one of the ten most decorative women in America but in the way millions of neighborhood matrons might be window-dressing in a lineup of female wrestlers or a women's auxiliary of the Mafia. I bathed once a day and dressed with care.

Carl had a small one-bedroom apartment in the Boyle Heights section of Los Angeles, two flights up. The building was neither new nor decrepit, the address nondescript. Ernest had phoned for the appointment and we were expected. Since I was a registered Communist by then, it had been agreed we would not make a point of my last name if the omission could be carried off unobtrusively. Carl, in slacks and sport shirt, introduced himself. So did Ernest, and Ernest turned to me.

"Marion, this is Carl Empey." Empey was not Carl's name.

"How do you do," said Carl. "I'm sorry, I didn't hear your last name."

My stupid action was reflex. I had forgotten we were not Communists. "Marion Marion," I said—and smirked.

"Really?" Carl was surprised. "Same last name as first?"

"Marion *Miller*," Ernest said sharply.

"Oh. I thought you said—"

"I misspoke. I was looking at your living room and wasn't thinking. How nice it is." Already I was babbling. It wasn't nice. It wasn't not nice. It was a furnished apartment.

For a few minutes the conversation was desultory. Carl liked sports, as we knew, and Ernest led him carefully. He spoke in praise of Archie Moore and Jackie Robinson but also of Marciano and some other ball players, mavericks like Robinson—I don't know who, but white ones. He confined his frame of reference to abilities alone; there was no mention of color. When it was time to say it, he said:

"I imagine you know why we're here, Mr. Empey. We'd like you with us on our Committee work. We've heard quite a little about you. I don't want to press you but we'd be interested to know how you feel about it. About us, that is. The Committee and what it's trying to do."

"I know generally about it, yes," said Carl. "There's some kind of ruction going on. I don't know just what it is."

"I wouldn't call it a ruction," said Ernest evenly. "I think protest is a fair word. You know of the McCarran Act, of course. To us who are foreign born—I'm a Pole, by the way—it seems discriminatory. I don't have to tell you that it's designed to keep out Communists and to deport Communists now resident here. All the rest is a pious evasion. However, our objection is that it affects all other foreigners as well. We'd like to stop that from happening."

Carl leaned forward, courteous and attentive. "I have no convictions on the subject. Well, I do have one. I'd say offhand that anything designed to impede Communists is a good thing."

Ernest smiled and lit a cigarette. "You may be right. But do you mind if we don't get diverted for a minute. I'm still thinking of the foreign born. You yourself must surely be aware of what it is to be a minority race. You don't object to my introducing race?"

"Why should I?" said Carl. "Obviously I'm a Negro. And yes, I'm aware of what it's like. But I don't agree I'm diverting the conversation. You say the Communist threat is the root of what Congress is doing. You're right. *My* point is that that's a good root to have. Now where are we?"

"Where we began," said Ernest. "The many will suffer for the sins of the few. That's what concerns us downtown. That's why we want you and everyone like you on our side. I'll speak frankly. We don't want simply your silent support, we want the hope that you'll get out and work. Try to forget the Communists, won't you? All seventeen of them, or however many there are in this country. Whenever I read of the so-called Communist threat, as I seem to every day of my life, I'm reminded of a piece of doggerel from my childhood. How does it go? 'Shut the door, they're coming through the window! Shut the window, they're coming through the door!' Something like that."

"But it's so true," said Carl.

Won't you come into my parlor? Ernest smiled again. "Mr. Empey, if I were any kind of salesman, I'd jump in your lap at this point, damn every Communist son-of-a-bitch who ever lived, and hand you a fountain pen and a bill of sale. But I'm not a salesman. I'm a lawyer. I read all the fine print and I think and think and I don't give a hoot in hell for majority opinion *as* majority opinion. Don't misunderstand me. I'm a patriot as you are a patriot. I'm an American before I'm a Pole. But I can't, I just can't, embrace the idea that if I like caviar or order vodka at a bar, I'll be visited next day by a ruddy-cheeked, cleft-chinned specimen of manhood from the FBI and told to pack my bag and get out of the country. That may be an unpopular point of view but it's mine."

"But they wouldn't do that," said Carl, who hadn't noticed that Ernest had sidestepped the issue Carl had launched—nor would I have noticed it if I hadn't been ready for it. "The FBI's not a fascist organization."

"Not in practice, certainly not. But in conception, wouldn't you say that it is? For example, does it make you happy that a law enforcement agency can go around asking questions about you of your friends and acquaintances? Not to mention enemies? And on no more grounds than an anonymous letter from some disgruntled landlord who doesn't like the way one of your visitors parts his hair. I can't honestly say it makes *me* happy. Tell you the truth, it scares me."

Carl's face seemed to harden a little. "It shouldn't. Unless you have something to be scared *of*. You haven't, have you?"

Ernest laughed this time. "Mr. Empey, I'm a corporation lawyer and, I think, a successful one. Have you ever heard of a corporation lawyer who was a Communist? I take it you *are* implying I'm a Communist."

Under his light brown skin, Carl flushed. "I beg your pardon, if you think that. I wasn't implying it. I thought this was an academic discussion."

"And of course it is," said Ernest swiftly. "And I beg *your* pardon for jumping at a silly conclusion. I guess the political climate of today makes us all jumpy. What actually I meant to say was that I'm nervous over the idea of anything, in this country, resembling the gestapo."

"Or the MVD."

"I wouldn't know about that," said Ernest. "I've never been to Russia."

"Neither have I. Anyway, we're talking into the wind. There's nothing police-state about the FBI."

"I hope not," said Ernest. "Let me get back to our political climate of today instead. That more than anything is what disturbs my sleep. As I've said, or maybe just suggested, I'm not violently anti-Communist. Not yet anyway. To my mind, the returns aren't all in. I don't mind saying that to someone like you, but I feel that if I said it to some casual gathering of upright American voters, I'd be lynched on the spot. What an ugly word, lynched. I hope you don't mind it."

"No. I'm West Indian, you know, not Deep South. But if I were Deep South, I still wouldn't mind it. It's a fact of life. The Negro in Mississippi who winked at the white woman. For that matter, the Scottsboro boys."

"Yes. The Scottsboro boys. As a lawyer, I can still get sore about that. But they did have a lot of friends working for them, you'll have to admit that. Just the same, it was one hell of a raw deal."

"They were doing pretty well, with Leibowitz and all. They were getting somewhere till the Communist Party came along and bitched it up. The Reds didn't care about those guys. They cared about the big, fat Communist cause, not a thing else. Soon as they waved that hammer and sickle, the Scottsboro boys were as good as dead."

"Not dead."

"They might as well have been."

"A shame," said Ernest, rather sweepingly. "A shame from beginning to end. And it brings us around again to what I call a majority political climate. Let a screenwriter depict an employer as an unpleasant person and socko!—these days he goes on a blacklist and can't get a job. Let a program on radio or television discuss or show a filthy, verminous apartment and the producer's 'un-American,' whatever that may mean. You have writing ambitions, haven't you, Mr. Empey? Well, you'll be interested in this: a screenwriter friend of mine suggested to a studio head one day last week that the writers' guild, his guild, be the final arbiters on each movie script, rather than the studio. It seemed sound to him and, I may as well add, it seems sound to me. Who would know writing better than writers? The semi-literate slob who happens to hold the pursestrings? You and I know better. But do you know what happened to him? He was ordered from the man's office and called a lousy Russian. How must it make our friends the Russians feel toward us, having the word 'lousy' prefixed to their nationality, their country, as a matter of patriotic American habit?" Ernest had stumbled and knew it but he did not permit himself to stammer on his error. Urbanely instead he backed up on the next sentence. "I said 'our friends.' I should have said co-existers."

Carl, I thought, was thawing under the deference of Ernest's manner, but he clung bravely to his hatred. "You may be right about our political climate," he said, "and God knows, I have nothing against Russians. Not for being Russians. But for my money, the Communists are still bastards and they'll always be bastards." He sat up sharply. "Excuse me, Miss Miller. Or is it Mrs.?"

"Mrs." I'd been silent so long I half-expected a liberated moth to fly out of me. "It's all right. Speak freely."

Ernest said, chuckling: "Bastards they may be. I envy your having conquered your doubts on the subject—or any subject. Doubt can be sheer torture and usually is. It's the curse of what we in this country call liberals."

"One thing sure," said Carl, "Communists have nothing to do with that. They're the liberal's worst enemy."

"There I disagree. Not to defend Communists, but the liberals' worst enemy are liberals. There I give you a sniveling lot of do-gooders who can't seem to get around to doing anything good. Or doing anything else. Let a working stiff be stretched on the rack, larcenous rent, a foreman who'll beat the poor guy's brains out so the foreman'll make his quota, nothing to work for but death, and what do the liberals do? Cry and write letters to the editor. And write a post script saying, 'Of course, the foreman, he has kids, too.' Let one businessman steal another blind in what we call so proudly the stimulus of competition, the American Way, and the liberal yells to stick him in jail and figures that settles everything. Never once does he question the nobility of competition itself. Name me a single liberal who has a good word to say for everyone pulling together toward one end, not cutting each other's throats. You can't because no liberal's ever said it."

Suddenly Ernest snapped his head up and put a wrist over his eyes. His face had become flushed and he had overplayed his hand. Now he tried to recover. "All the same, Mr. Empey, the sins of collectivism may be all you say they are. Who am I, a filthy capitalist of a corporation lawyer, to say they aren't?" He took his wrist away. "It's hard for you and me to understand how a Hollywood fat cat can sit by his swimming pool and curse the system that gives him three thousand dollars a week for making a public exhibition of his own fat-headedness, his willingness to be a whore, and his—well, political immaturity. Yet when a guy comes out of a mine shaft spitting blood and thinks there might be some other way to run things . . . Oh, hell, I don't know. Let's have a moratorium on political ideologies and get back to the Committee. That's what Marion and

I are here for. Can you look on the Reds as a drop in the bucket
and think of the thousands of innocents who are being discrim-
inated against? I'll tell you what we'll do, you and I. We'll
stand on the dock by the unloading gate and pole-axe every
Commie who comes down the ramp, like cattle." His laugh was
avuncular and rich, full of good will.

As a dissertation, it had not left me unimpressed. The last
part especially had left an imprint, since I recognized it—the
bit about the Hollywood fat cat and the miner—as having been
stolen piecemeal from a book I'd read not long before, Ludwig
Bemelmans' *Dirty Eddie.* The sole difference had been that
Ernest had reversed Bemelmans' order of emphasis, thus chang-
ing the whole intent. Bemelmans had had his character, a vivid
anti-Communist, speak first of the miner, *then* of the fat cat.
Bemelmans' thus had been an anti-Communist dissertation in
itself. Now with a flip of the card, Ernest had switched the
point of view so the Communist slant had the all-important
closing lick.

For the next hour there was no invasion by Ernest of possibly
dangerous terrain. So benevolent had he become that I was
brought into the discussion, the way for my modest forensics
smoothly paved by Ernest. Carl did not say he would join the
Committee in its anti-McCarran efforts, but assuredly he did
not say he wouldn't. Plainly he liked Ernest and was impressed
by him. More plainly he was dazzled by the promise of playing
Don Quixote to the stolid, stupid windmills of the masses.
Ernest had so manipulated his pitch—so skillful the right pressure on the right nerve. Morris would have applauded.

Six days later Ernest reported to headquarters that Carl had
agreed to join the Committee as an active member and in particular as a worker against the McCarran Act. At home that

night I told Paul of Ernest's call, and that meant Paul would put into execution the plan we had agreed on.

Paul phoned Carl and in a rough, disguised voice told him he knew of his negotiations with Ernest, that Ernest was among the three most dangerous Communists on the West Coast and that Carl was being suckered by a master. Carl cursed and hung up on him. Doggedly Paul called again. "Please don't hang up this time. Hear what I have to say. If I'm lying, you'll find out and I'll come over there and let you beat the —— out of me. I won't even raise a hand. Now will you listen?"

Carl listened—the real urgency in Paul's voice was something no one but a Communist could hang up on. Paul has a fount of Red information, he's a handbook on the national operation, and he read Carl dates and places on Ernest, citing names and evidence that Carl could check once he had been given the leads.

I waited anxiously for the outcome but at headquarters for several days nothing was said. Then on a Thursday morning there was a squib in one of the papers that Ernest R., well-known local attorney, had been severely beaten in his office by a Negro youth identified by police as Carl Empey of x address. At the office I learned next day that Ernest had withdrawn charges, but had left word with me that Carl, while he would not seek me out, would knock me down on sight, woman or no woman. I never saw him again and I guess, since I have yet to be knocked down by a man, he never saw me.

So Carl cut down Ernest's batting average a little, but Ernest fattened it again with his next prospect. I sat in on that deal, too, and it was Carl all over again, save that the man's name was Leo (only it wasn't) and he was Teutonic. And he was old enough for failure to have jelled for him. After our first session, he reviled us both for Communist "predilection." Yet a month later he became a Party member, after another warning by Paul. The old con may not be an ICBM but it has long-range uses of its own still, so long as the nerve remains exposed and the pressure is willing, ever willing, to be exerted again and again and again.

Incidentally, Ernest was lying when he told Carl he'd never been in Russia. He was trained in Moscow for a year and a half just before World War II. I don't know whether that makes any difference or not.

11

One Communist

AMERICAN COMMUNISTS I HAVE KNOWN ARE AS a whole a chatty lot but not often on the subject of their own lives. This must stem from the furtive nature of the enterprise itself, since they are not sparing of the word "I". It's just the autobiographical details that choke them up, and I suspect a psychiatrist might have a difficult time eliciting a case history.

One, though, from the very first weeks of my apprenticeship, sought in me a mother confessor and for all the years thereafter told me of himself in bits and pieces, frequently lubricated by double bourbons on the rocks. Intemperate drinking is by no means common among the brotherhood, though one very prominent Los Angeles Red is a known alcoholic. His present wife was ordered by the Party to marry him in order to keep him away from the jug. This presented problems—she had to divorce an incumbent husband to get around to him, for instance—and the trickiest of them was that the alcoholic hated her so thoroughly he promptly guzzled himself into a sanitarium where he was restrained by straps from getting up and killing her.

Hubert, the man I came to know by way of his own unin-

vited confidences, did not drink like this but the bottle made
him voluble all the times it did not sink him into a state resembling manic depression. I never gathered the idea that he
intended his revelations to prove anything, yet in the end perhaps they did. As a non-psychologist, I will not rule on that.
If you wish to, you certainly may.

Hubert was forty-two when I met him, forty-seven when the
Party and I ceased making discordant music together. He was
born in Brooklyn of parents whose last name was as native as
Perkins, attended the public schools there, and got his degree
from a large and justly famous Manhattan university. He had
one brother, older than he, and grew up under his domination.
The liquid Hubert was given to self-pity but his contention
that the brother had a sadistic streak recurred so frequently
that I'm inclined to think it may be so. Either that or he simply
couldn't stand Hubert.

When Hubert was in his mid-teens, he suffered an accident
to his nervous system that left one corner of his mouth pulled
upward in the shape of a mirthless leer, as a stroke might have
done. This mishap made his appearance not so much ugly as
grotesque, drawing stares and a certain degree of withdrawal
on the part of his male contemporaries and curtailing whatever
girl-life he might have had. Hubert's twisted mouth was nowhere near so appalling as he thought, any more than the name
Hubert was as comic and undignified as he thought. But the
point was, he thought these things. The reality was irrelevant.

As I understand the aftermath, Hubert's unhappy self-con-
sciousness caused him to turn inward on himself and in time
created an imbalance. He kept to himself increasingly, read
anything and everything he could get his hands on, and began
at the age of seventeen to write in seriousness, whereas prior to
his illness he had written merely because that seemed to be

his knack. He had been quite a luminary on the high school year book and was an even greater luminary on his campus newspaper. He had a touch of genius for a feathery, light-hearted sort of prose—strange in a man whose heart was heavier than most—and in his junior year at the university sold two short stories to one national magazine and a third to another. After that he collected a dozen rejection slips in a row and reacted very badly—not according to him, but as disclosed by his way of telling it. I know nothing of paranoia besides the dictionary definition but I am reasonably sure that editors of national repute were not turning down Hubert's stories because of office jealousy or bugaboos having to do with low reader I.Q. As late as 1950, Hubert still thought that was it.

He was alone now almost all the time. He had lost the facility for social give and take and when he lost it, he decided quite defensively that he didn't want it anyway.

Hubert graduated into the barren 1930's, sponged off his mother and father for seven months, and then very luckily, through the intervention of a college friend, got a job on a newspaper in a large Eastern seaboard city at thirty dollars a week. His campus reputation as a journalist spared him the intermediate step of copy boy and he was put immediately on general assignment. It was good that this break came when it did, since his older brother had beaten him up three days before. There was no clear reason for it except "I'm sick of seeing you sit around here on your ass." The older brother was running numbers for Dutch Schultz.

On the paper at first Hubert stayed shyly and morosely away from the others on the city desk but finally warmed a bit to two or three of them and drank with them after hours—now and then during hours—at a bar around the corner. The men toward whom he had gravitated, toward whose personality he was drawn, were hyperactive members of the American Newspaper Guild in a paper that was still an open shop. It was their wish and that of the ANG to tie it up. Hubert had no political consciousness at that time but wished to please his two or three friends and became a passive Guild member. At the third Guild meeting he attended, however, he found himself excited over the directional trend toward increased Guild authority over employment practices, and actually made a speech. In the months to come, he became in the order of their appearance here, a devoted admirer of Franklin Roosevelt, the paper's star feature writer, and a rabid disciple of Heywood Broun, a splendid newspaperman who loved labor more dearly than he loved dogs.

As Hubert worked on and honed, because it could not be otherwise, his light prose touch until it became sprightly and sometimes downright brilliant, his salary mounted. In 1940 he was making $75 a week; in 1941, $90. That was good money then in the circles wherein Hubert moved. The Japanese did what they did on December 7 of that year. In late February of 1942 Hubert was turned down by the military for psychoneurosis, and the next fall he was made a local columnist. That put him up to one-twenty-five, and lessened his interest in the Guild. At thirty-four, Hubert was by no means ready to explore selflessness. Being conductor of a column, however, did not compensate Hubert for not being in uniform. Although he realized much later that his true feeling was one of relief, he suffered then terrible guilt agonies and for a while went about wearing in his lapel a ruptured duck he had borrowed from a friend, invalided out, who wanted no part of it. One night the eventuality that really he had feared most all along came about: a uniformed serviceman, well oiled, beat him up in a bar for being a goddam 4-F. Three days later his Guild activities resumed their feverish pace as though they had never slacked.

The first three friends he had made, two military over-age and one strangely effeminate who said the army had rejected him for lung scars, had by then in beery conclave stated to Hubert they were Communists, and while the word shocked him, for it still carried shock impact, he was excited by such daring and listened intently to what they had to say. When the Hitler-Stalin pact was made, the effeminate man screamed drunkenly and threw his Guild card down a sewer, but the other two rationalized the move. When Hitler attacked Russia and Russia fought grimly back, Stalin and friends suddenly were not dirty words any more.

Hubert, while not prepared to take so dizzying a step as Party membership, became as noisy at Guild meetings as his friends and sometimes noisier. At the same time, although his physical defect was as pronounced as ever, he thrust a cautious head out of the tent of his timidity and allowed himself a violent love affair with a woman several years older than he. Its end was disastrous and Hubert cut one wrist mildly with a dull razor blade, phoning a friend a minute afterward to come a-running with tourniquets. After that Hubert became almost, if not quite, as reclusive as he had been at college. In addition he began drinking alone in his room. He found he liked it. He even had drinks a few times in the morning when he got up feeling extra bad. He liked that, too.

In the summer of 1944, one of Hubert's columns was killed, thrown out by the managing editors, the first time it had happened. It was a column in headlong praise of Roosevelt and acidly disparaging both to the Republican candidate and the Republican party behind him. Hubert threw what, in a girl, would have been called a tantrum. The managing editor heard him out coldly and informed him that the paper still was being run by the man who owned it and this man happened to be a Republican. Hubert not only had conniptions but made a speech at the next Guild meeting that upset even his Communist friends. They explained to him later that the overthrow of publishers would come, all right, but all in due time and please not to shout about it until the word was sent down from higher places. In September of that year an advertiser who spent hundreds of thousands of dollars with the paper objected to another column of Hubert's and that involved not only a kill but a retraction as well, plus a dressing down from the publisher personally. For the first time in his life that night, Hubert employed the word facist in reference to a democratic American.

Hubert's opposite number, so to speak, on the paper wrote a column more somber than Hubert's and in a style rather less slick, but the man was an adroit internal politician and besides had a greater following than Hubert. The paper had for quite a while been considering offering this man for syndication and in 1945, in conjunction with a great newspaper chain, he was so offered. Hubert was staggered, sick with pain that it had not happened to him. He began systematically to hate the other columnist, a big Irishman who was years senior to Hubert and always friendly to him, and to pray for the column's speedy demise. When this did not occur, Hubert began approaching his own column with no more appetite than a dyspeptic approaches an early breakfast, and this became obvious in the finished product. His readership slacked off, his mail slacked off, he lost weight and, shortly after the Japanese had decided Hiroshima was more than enough, he lost his job.

There was an indignation meeting with his Communist friends, abetted by three imports from New York, and these told him that he simply was a victim of caprice, grasping advertisers and the capitalistic system, that under Communism it never could have happened. A year before Hubert had considered them squirrely in a harmless and inconsequential way. Now he listened very hard and his ears flapped a bit.

With the money he had saved and his severance pay, he went to ground in his room and wrote an irate, cathartic and inept novel, which somehow found a cheapjack publisher and even more astoundingly spent six precarious weeks on the list of ten best sellers. One of the New York Party members who had talked to him earlier got him in touch with a New York agent who had four or five good Hollywood connections, and pretty soon Hubert's book had been sold to the movies. So had Hubert, at $750 a week with all kinds of ominous looking options. Hubert fought his way past the options, however, option by option, and by late 1948 was able to free-lance at a set price of $40,000 a script. He found that one script a year was plenty for his well-being, two practically redundant.

He bought a ranch house and had a pool installed but he was not at all happy. He was on the edge of being wretched. Nobody ever recognized his name except in the industry, no matter how many screen credits he had, and the writing of films provided him with little more mental or spiritual nourishment than eclairs after eighteen holes of golf. Most of the studios he sold wouldn't even let him on the set of his own picture. He had plenty of money and nowhere to go and nothing to do, and when he fell in love with a thin, homely woman, twice divorced, with overwhelming political convictions and a way of making him feel like a great man, he married her in a hurry.

She was a strident Communist who ran an *avant garde* art gallery, and her friends were Communists or so nearly Communists that there was no appreciable difference. They fussed over Hubert and he warmed his hands on what seemed to be their genuine affection. He had not felt this way since he had gone with a drunk friend to a number of meetings of Alcoholics Anonymous, whose tolerance for human frailty is virtually infinite and who for a while catered to Hubert under the impression, which he did not discourage, that he himself was alcoholic. He wasn't, but he had found it a wondrous thing to be able to have a few drinks and then phone various AA members with his spurious pleas for help. Obediently they would come to him, whatever the hour, and talk gravely and understandingly and it gave Hubert not just the glow of their solicitude but likewise a feeling of power. The AAs grew shortly to understand and disbelieve him, and left him severely alone, whatever his yowls; but he couldn't forget the good feeling. His wife's Communist friends gave it to him again.

When he went to his first Party meeting, he experienced the same reactions, although the people struck him as several cuts below the arrested alcoholics with their gentle Christianity and cheerful compassion. Hubert of course had this pseudo-Communist background of his own and did not believe for a moment the stories of steel discipline and bestial vindictiveness. Also, he loved his wife or thought he did. He became a registered Communist on the fourth day of the sixth decade of the century, snapped to attention for orders, and wrote into his next film script a scene totally out of context, featuring the abilities of a poor but honest doctor.

This doctor had been ministering, in return for nothing but gifts of food, to the needs of workers in the factory of a rapacious villain named Van something. The workers, cruelly underpaid, raised these vegetables and fruits in their own gardens. The villainous factory owner's wife, herself a parasitic sort bulbous in mink, fell critically ill and was about to be done in by a quack surgeon with a Cadillac convertible when the poor but honest medic brushed him aside and himself completed the operation successfully. When the wife came out of the sodium pentothal, her words, looking up at p. but h., were: "Now—I see everything." The workers all were given raises and shares in the company totaling fifty-one per cent—and Hubert returned to his story line, which had to do, aside from this strange intrusion, with backstage goings-on in a Broadway musical. Hubert's peculiar flight into another world died on the producer's desk, and after that script Hubert got no writing jobs except from wild and mysterious young men in independent production who talked furiously of witch hunts and the sacredness of one's convictions. And there weren't many of these gentry around.

This debacle made Hubert something less than useful to the Party until it hit on the idea of having him write its propaganda material, both as pamphlets and through the medium of its various undernourished newspapers.

Hubert grew restive that autumn and tried to break away, but his loneliness was too much. His friends, as he told me, had ordered a truckload of ten-foot poles just to be sure to have something not to touch him with, and there was nobody else anywhere. He was intermittently reassured by Party slaps on the back and the admonishments that under Communism— *der tag* was not far off—talent would be rewarded in direct ratio to its capacity, no matter what filthy lies were disseminated by capitalism under phony Moscow date-lines. Hubert hoped so hard this was true that he came to believe it.

In the early 1930's he had been terrifically moved by a motion picture version of the Marcel Pagnol play *Topaze*, the sequence in which Professor Topaze awarded the classroom prize for—what? composition?—to the poor, deserving boy over the head of the rich little loafer whose father had tried to pull strings. Hubert couldn't remember the exact words but roughly Professor Topaze, played with great impressement by the late John Barrymore, had said to the winner: "Try to remember when you grow up that once, just once, the prize did go to the person who won it. The race *did* go to the swift." Or maybe he said it to the whole class. Was M. Pagnol a Communist? Hubert's question was eager. I didn't know. I had never heard of M. Pagnol.

When I saw Hubert, in 1955, he was haggard and somewhat unkempt. Many days he was slightly unshaven, just enough to make his appearance forbidding. His eyes were always strained and wistful, and he seemed lost. He looked like a man who had been cheated but couldn't figure how or where or by whom. He was diligent as ever in his Party work but in the manner of someone who simply didn't know what else to do. He said to me once while drinking, "The days are so goddam long, Marion. I don't know where I'm going and the lousiest part of all, I don't know where I've been. I look back on the road and all I see is litter and debris. What the hell's wrong with everybody?"

That's the point where Hubert always used to start to cry. I picked up both our checks and got out of there. So they sent Ernest to talk to Hubert. You remember Ernest. And after that, I never again heard Hubert express uncertainty of any kind, and he became a very "good" Communist indeed and does not drink any more. The Party told him if he did, he would be kicked out for keeps. Today, the last thing Hubert would want is that. He grows unhappier as he grows more vicious; he cannot eject his poison as fast as it fills up in him. But after his fashion, he is a very good soldier.

12

Credo

DURING THE FIRST QUARTER OF THIS YEAR, A MAN very prominent in the entertainment industry employed as a writer a notorious figure whose notoriety sprang from his refusal to tell a Congressional committee whether he was or ever had been a member of the Communist Party.

There was considerable public indignation over this move, the usual letters to the editor and the customary threats to boycott then and there and forever more any enterprise with which the employer might be connected in the future. That kind of public indignation is laudable but unfortunately short-lived, nor is its impact greater than the impact of any three-day wonder. In fact, the employer could, if he wished, point to precedent. A colleague of this writer's and a fellow defier of Congressional authority already was back earning money at his trade. He indeed was, a few days after the unholy alliance I have already mentioned, reinstated to full grace by his guild. This came on the heels of his being hired, as the first writer was, to do a job of work for Hollywood. There was no concealment about either move, though prior to their happening, the second writer had been functioning under an assumed name. So, for all I know, had the first.

As I say, the chorus of public indignation over both moves was laudable. But I think it would have been much firmer and longer lasting if the citizens who got sore for a few minutes had had access to certain background information. I have access to this. To the best of my knowledge and belief, moreover, my information is rooted in fact. The nature of my work for the FBI linked me to sources I have never relinquished, sources who make it their business to study the convolutions of the Communist Party as closely as scientific instruments track an unseen satellite. If these were not at work, the layman wouldn't know whether Sputnik was coming or going. More disquieting, he probably wouldn't care.

To help make the point I want so badly to make in this chapter, it is well to begin with the character and temperament of the two men who did the hiring. I do not know personally either them or their hirelings, but this is hardly relevant. Our scientists have never poked around the Sputniks either.

The man who first employed openly a renegade citizen of the United States against a turbulent climate of Hollywood opinion is a fellow of surly, Teutonic temperament. He allegedly beats his head against walls when crossed. Like the other man, the more famous one whose story begins this chapter, he would seem to take a perverse pleasure in championing an unpopular position. Earlier in his career, he swam against the current of motion picture censorship to make a film that was hardly worth the swim. A later picture of his, while enjoying kudos, still employed language that could easily have been avoided without lessening the film's impact. A newspaperman friend of mine who has interviewed him at some length doubts the sincerity of the man's purpose. He sounded to my friend merely like a guy who wanted to start something, a child setting off a firecracker at a tea party. His natural metier, my friend said, is the metier of trouble, and he seeks martyrdom as fiercely as a salmon battling its way upstream to spawn. As for another motivation, my friend points out, this man—who is no longer an actor—hires a full-time press agent. Persons indifferent to publicity for publicity's sake do not hire full-time press agents.

The second and more spectacular employer was said once by an intimate of his to have been born not with a chip on his shoulder but a whole tree. Since he is slight of build, this estimate can be reduced to sapling. He hired his "unfriendly witness" in his, the employer's, role of independent producer. When he was criticized, as inevitably he was, he raised the two issues that by now have become familiar to the point of reader ennui. One was that it was nobody's business whom he hired, the second that political outlook had nothing to do with film writing. Uh-huh. Having then committed himself to a specific attitude and course of action, he could not back down. That is true: psychologically, this particular man seemed incapable of backing down. He would regard such a course of conduct as "chicken"—in his early environment, an epithet of unbearable contempt.

There is a story, authenticated, that this celebrity of whom I am still talking once knocked a man down at a party for a fancied insult, hospitalizing him in the process. His victim on this occasion was not the first person he had flattened by any means but he was the first to have been seriously hurt. A lawsuit was threatened with its complement of adverse publicity, and the slugger finally was persuaded to apologize. With ill grace, he went to the man's hospital room, but the apology choked him. He was able only to thrust out his hand and say, "Hah yuh doin'?" That was the extent of it. The lawsuit was forestalled due to the injured man's forgiveness, not any good grace on the attacker's part.

This almost legendary person has a long, well-documented record as a militant advocate of, let us say, liberal views. His feeling for the underdog is ferocious, often unreasoning and probably sincere. His friends say he is barely capable of clarity of thought. His ultimate responses are tears of anger or fists. For all his wealth and fame, he is believed by those best qualified to know to be insecure and frightened. He is seldom without an entourage of a dozen sycophants, and advisers whose advice he does not take. His name has appeared in the records of Government hearings on Communist influence. He is afraid of Germans, all Germans, and has frequently said so, but never so often or so loudly as when Moscow's anti-German line became vociferous.

That this man should be in fact a Communist sympathizer is beyond belief to thinking persons. His income is and has been for years enormous, he perhaps could not survive in a socialistic state, and his side-interests have a very capitalistic flavor indeed. Yet—for all I know, unwittingly on his part—he is a favorite of the Communist Party. They think—and this I do know—that they'll get him some day. Meanwhile, he is playing patsy for them beyond their fondest hopes. People like him, whose emotions outweigh the cerebral processes so emphatically, always have in them the stuff of Communist patsys.

I do not believe he's a Communist or a fellow-traveler—yet —and neither does the Party. The thing is, he doesn't have to be. He is wonderfully useful to the comrades right where he is, in this condition of pugnacity and vacillation. As a Party member, he might prove a drag. He would, for example, be subject to Party discipline, which would circumvent his activities severely. Besides that, he would run the risk of exposure, which would wash him up in the entertainment industry and so foreclose to a great extent his Party usefulness. But as a free agent, not fellow-traveling but at least traveling in the same general direction, he is worth his weight in rubles.

Let us take his hiring of the writer who will not say he's *not* a Communist.

I have reason to believe—and this is infinitely more than idle hearsay—that the Communist Party of the United States worked for a solid year to bring this hiring about. I want to think that the famous man does not know that, that he may be reading about it here for the first time. My information is that it was done by the Party's most skilled persuaders, working undercover and through intermediaries. I am told, by someone who in this area of politics makes it a vocation to know what he's talking about, that the hiring itself was all part of a package: the Party's long-range end is to restore to grace all those writers whose reticence before Congress got them in hot water. The Teuton who supposedly beats his head against walls was their first success. The Great Man was their second—and a dilly!

The persuaders, I am told—the man I have called "Ernest" was among them—got to the Great Man with an unremitting, indirect assault on several vulnerable fronts. It was brought deviously to his attention that the writer was in bad personal straits. He was reminded somehow that kicking a man when he is down is not the American way. The Great Man was read chapter and verse on the number of his enemies—and the Great Man has as many as does any contentious man—who were opposed to the writer. He was reminded time and again of the inviolability of the thought processes. He was informed in so many words that the writer was *not* a Communist, he was just a guy standing up for the rights of freedom and refusing to blow the whistle on his friends.

No sensitive area the Great Man was known to possess was left untouched. It is even to the Great Man's credit that he held out as long as he did. But he gave in at last—and then backed down! For a miracle, he reconsidered. He rescinded his hiring, or at any rate did so on record. What prompted him? Public pressure, you say. But this man, doesn't he get his kicks from spitting in the eye of public pressure? Economic reasons, then. But isn't this man rich? Then why the *volte-face?* It was more out of character than the hiring itself. I don't know why the *volte-face.* It could have been that the writer's work had been completed. The Great Man wanted to have his cake and eat it, too.

Right from the start, two things were flagrantly apparent. One was that the writer was by no means an indispensable man where the writing of the proposed script was concerned. He was pretty good but he wasn't that good. On the other hand, there were available dozens of better writers identified with the right wing of politics, writers outspokenly anti-Communist, who for some reason are finding it hard to get work these days. These were passed over.

It was disconcerting also to know that the book the writer was called on to adapt for films was a book harshly critical by inference of the United States Army and its administration. From the Communist standpoint, their boy was just the lad to do it. And maybe he is.

I don't want to be wholly uncharitable to this celebrated stooge I have called the Great Man. I want to apply to him the kindest word in this situation I can muster. He's a fathead.

There is a purpose to the foregoing much more serious than churning up a trivia of Hollywood gossip. Hollywood has its place here, it is true, but only in the sense of its importance as a communications area. The Communists, you will have read before, would dearly like to get a foot into the communications area, followed if possible by every other inch of the anatomy. Of course they would. Invade the minds and prejudices of man and perhaps there will be no need ever to fire a missile.

Does anyone think Fidel Castro, with a ragtag army of a few thousand, won a military victory in Cuba? He won because the people wanted him to win; that is, they wanted Batista to lose. The people are what counts, the public will. *You* are the people. Please bear it in mind. The Communists do. The Communists doubt now that they can bring about a revolution without enough of the people, rightly positioned. They know as well that they could not consolidate their victory without the same support. (Once the consolidation is accomplished, hang onto your hat. You won't matter then. But that's something else.)

During the five years I was intimate with the Communist Party and its processes, it underwent a change in strategy whose end I cannot yet foresee. I can only say that, to my distress, they finally began going about their plans in a way that made sense. They finally became *dangerous* to America—and that danger increases every day.

No longer can a thinking person laugh off what once was a bobtail fringe of misfits. Now there's trouble for us, and it can get to be worse trouble. Believe me, believe me, *believe me!*— you *must* take them seriously.

The words I say to you now are not only mine. *They are likewise the words of top Communist planners.* I have sat with them in strategic sessions, at a level near enough to the top so that in effect it was the top. *I have been there.* That statement comprises my credentials.

As recently as 1949, a thinking American could be excused

for not taking the Communist "threat" seriously. In that year I did not myself agree with the segment of opinion that held we all were fools for not waking to the peril. It was no use for the big newspaper empires to hammer at me. I wanted to see what Dagwood was doing.

For one thing, Moscow was thousands of miles away and as remote as Babylon. For another, when I did look around me here at home, I could see only a passel of maladjusted fools making incomprehensible noises.

From a semantics standpoint alone, their public relations were atrocious. The seediest press agent in Hollywood or New York or Grand Rapids could have set them straight. They insisted, to begin with, on the word "Communist," a major semantic error. The conditioned reflex of America to "Communist" is a punch in the nose.

In Los Angeles, which can serve as an index to the rest of the country, their spoken pitch was as frowsy as ever—wild-eyed, unattractive men and women screaming over the heads of disinterested stragglers in Pershing Square—in New York, Union Square. Their raffish and impecunious newspapers were strident and angry beyond belief—the hard sell was running away with the bit in its teeth. How could any of us get nervous?

Then one day understanding came to them. New high level conferences began. The voices were quiet. In gentle, unobtrusive fashion, the atmosphere of "big time" settled over the meeting. For the big time was what they were shooting at.

The word "Communist" was retired to the background. The park orators were toned down or done away with. The Party ceased to talk in rotund terms of the size of its membership; on the contrary, it began to go along with estimates that there weren't many of them. The new strategic blueprint came down from Moscow. Someone in the Kremlin, despite a popular belief to the contrary, knows something about the workings of the American mind.

Communist leaders I have heard have got around to acknowledging that Communism is not popular here. That did not hurt their feelings, it simply dictated the change of tack that today veers near to us and rocks our boat.

How much more effective, the leaders reasoned, might their approaches be if they were made in the lowest of tones and *through the mouths not of Communists but of influential spokesmen for the American scene.* Was there not a way of manipulating the wires so that even these spokesmen, were they ideologically opposed to the movement, were unaware of who the puppeteers were? Of course there was a way. An almost mystic chain of command was set in motion downward. Somewhere along the line the link between the original order and the voice that spoke the words—or wrote the words—was effectively obscured.

We speak of "fellow travelers" *much* too carelessly. It is a term with a wide range, and fellow travelers under the Communists' brave new world serve the cause as Communists never could and hard-core Americans never will. It is they who smudge the link so it becomes indecipherable, so that origins never can be traced back. They serve a cause most of them do not comprehend because they are fatheads, brilliant fatheads, influential fatheads, beguiling fatheads. Naturally a few know perfectly well what they're serving and may be said not to be fatheads but evil, twisted men. But most are infatuated fatheads, adolescents in love with a scheming dazzler who is not for them.

Listen to me, please! This is the new Communism in the United States. That is how it works. You see it all around you every day if only you *will* see it. And do not think of Communism that it can't happen here. It can—and if 180,000,000 of us don't snap out of it one of these days soon, it will. These enemies of ours, they *care*. They work for capitalism's overthrow night and day. We don't go to a union meeting or a neighborhood rally because we're tired and besides there's no place to park. Communists, who do not permit tiredness, park eight blocks away and walk. It is bad, as so often we are told, to be behind Russia in rocket and missile development. But to be behind the Communists in will, in wanting to, is a lot worse. Apathy and a full stomach, this combination is not good when someone is circling you with his eye on the jugular.

Is this new program of theirs getting anywhere? Sure it is. I will not say or even imply which of our prominent persons in the key areas of communications, labor and politics I think are Communists or Communist followers. But I know, and you know, some of those that *quack* like a duck.

The Great Man of entertainment I have written about and the head-banging Teuton, these quack like a duck.

Two world-famous nuclear scientists in our midst have quacked like a duck, and one of them does so habitually. (He was one of the sponsors of the Los Angeles Committee for Protection of Foreign Born, among his much lesser quacks.)

There is a television comedian of questing and confused intellect whose name from time to time appears on pronouncements I know have originated with the Party—and who meanwhile quacks like a duck on his own. If I may intrude a personal note here, this man has to Paul and me the simpering, superior air of one who considers his audience not really worthy of his talents, and this air is part and parcel of every infected Communist we ever have met. Paul in particular—and I have seen this proved out again and again—can spot a Communist as acutely as a pathologist can spot a homosexual, and he will bet our new car that the comedian is a Red weapon knowingly.

A TV commentator and interviewer, once widely seen and admired, has managed time and again to sound like a man who sounds like a Communist. His manner is engaging, his voice warm and trained, his supercilious manner rather well restrained, although he never has managed to bury it completely. His audience is tremendous—all in all, a far cry from the shaggy bum in the park who never got to first base except with those who were convinced anyway.

A widely-read newspaper columnist cannot seem to bring himself to speak unkindly of the Reds—or during all this year to stop needling Dwight Eisenhower. He is effective because he rarely editorializes—and the directive not to do that came right down from CP headquarters.

Thus to my knowledge, the new Communist offensive, the one that wears a necktie, combs its hair and speaks with modulation, has penetrated most successfully thus far into communications. The Party probes for its patsys before it moves in and this element has proved more susceptible than the other two. The emotions are closer to the surface, the adrenal system ejects peculiar waves to the brain, the heart bleeds when it is commanded to bleed.

Labor unions, those beloved objectives of wistful Communist stabs, have not fallen so easily—to the best of my knowledge, scarcely at all. There is a division of opinion in this country that believes our unions to be Communist dominated. A few of them are. But not the vast majority. Don't take my word for it. Take the word of those who ought to know, the high councilors of the Party. They are most unhappy that our labor continues to be *our labor*. Labor diligently has cleaned its own house, and continues to do so.

Government office will be Communism's end attainment. The

area cannot be assaulted directly; they haven't the votes. There is good reason to believe, too, that not many Alger Hisses have snuck in anywhere. But this should not provide too much re-assurance, inasmuch as the citadels of communications and labor are the battlefields. If these should fall, government sooner or later simply would drop into the Party's lap, and then everything would be over. Sooner, I might add, than later.

I could not have come out of five years of Communist affilia-tion and counterespionage without a credo of my own. But it doesn't have to be a long one. It is this:

Watch it. Watch yourself. They're wearing sneakers now in-stead of hobnail boots. They don't scream, "Banzai!" the way they once did before they charge. They're moving in from the side, out of ambush. They used to be a little absurd. They're not any more. They're under the bed. It's a fact.

Don't shrug. You must care. You *must.*

No, they're no longer in very plain view. And they are patient, patient as the years. You have a lifetime. They have many lifetimes, all the generations it might take. Now they push to the front the masks they have captured and themselves stay back, hidden behind famous and respected faces. For their voices they have substituted the voices known to millions. But the words are theirs.

You can't laugh them off. There's nothing to laugh at. Capi-talist America is the last stronghold, yes, but they believe, the Communists, that no stronghold is impregnable. *I* believe that this one is—until the day it concludes that since it is impreg-nable, it need not be guarded. Remember Singapore in World War II, the mightiest defenses in the world—and every one facing the sea? And the enemy came in from the back, and it was all over before Winston Churchill could call down his thunder of contempt on the little brown men, almost before one British planter could say to another, "One more lump, please." What bastion of empire ever could be so mighty as to forget there is a back door? What single nation could ever be so powerful as to allow itself the luxury of indifference?

Well, this one could. And it is allowing itself just that.

I am not brilliant, I am not a sage, I am not a strategist. But I have one asset to place at my country's disposal. I have been behind the enemy lines, right smack in his HQ. And I came back. I have been told that in war such a returnee might well be beyond price. I am properly overwhelmed. I know that as Marion Miller, I am a long way from priceless. But as a lucky accident, I may have some worth—if people will hear me.

In Santa Monica, the city just west of us, on the bluff overlooking the Pacific Ocean, there is a public park. The only hitch to it is that that bluff has a way of disengaging itself in bits and pieces and falling two or three hundred feet on to the Coast Highway. That way the strollers or picnickers stand a fair chance of being killed. Santa Monica has gone so far toward acknowledging the danger as to post little signs setting forth the nature of the hazard and adding as a kind of afterthought that you're there at your own risk. It's always reminded me of the restaurants and parking lots that disclaim all responsibility for anything you may check with them. Santa Monica doesn't mind if you check your life but will be damned if they'll have anything to do with your losing it.

The thought that this may constitute a shrieking piece of civic irresponsibility concerns me only in passing. I do wish they'd seal off the park but since obviously they're not going to, I try for the next best thing and wish people would stop going there. That doesn't help either. They still go, every day of the year. This leaves me one more paltry wish—that they'd read the signs.

And never yet have I seen one person read them.

Oh, well. Even if they did, they would know perfectly well that bluff would never slide out from under *them*. Not *them*. How could it? Got a rock base, hasn't it?

Yes, it has. It has a rock base, and the geological fault that sends tons of that rock sliding off the bluff on an average of twice a year grows faultier, imperceptibly faultier, month after month after month.

One time four women playing canasta on the bluff's edge were dumped neatly all the way down to the highway, still in unbelieving paralysis holding their cards in neat fans. For an incredible miracle, not one was badly hurt. But suppose, as the engineers' odds later indicated, death had come to all four? Wouldn't at least one of them, on the way down, have had a fleeting moment of belated wonderment as to what it was the city had had printed on those cute little signs? Something about dogs on leashes, very likely.

For most people it's hard to believe even now that the signs say the bluff might come out from under you. That would be something out of Dick Tracy, much too ridiculous to credit.

Re-reading, I can see that my analogy is not perfect. It may even be somewhat strained, as analogies go.

I suppose, for instance, that the city of Santa Monica has its reasons for not sealing off an area it admits is dangerous, just as the United States Government has reason for not sealing off the Communist Party. But I do wish people would take the trouble to read signs and, having read them, heed them. Rock slides and Communists are not funny. Bringing forth their best efforts, they could not get a laugh from a euphoric child. The earth beneath us shifts and trembles, and when or if it should swallow us, the time will be too late to regret that you thought it was just a truck passing.

13

Loose Ends

ODDS AND ENDS OF UNREGURGITATED MEMORIES LIT-
ter my desk now. They are set down in my own notes, a species
of homemade shorthand that might easily baffle the crypto-
grapher who broke the Japanese code in wartime. "Splk Rosemary N. dig bomb bit pow!" Well, pow to *you*, Rosemary N.
I haven't the faintest idea what I had in mind. "No picket but
shove black coffee. Check." Check what? But here is one plain
as the nose on Harry Bridges' face. "Kaput Viola, the tight little
aisle awaits." A cinch.

Viola was a woman of British birth, one of four Los Angeles
Communists facing deportation. One of these was a writer who
had a following of a kind in the arts. Another was a Korean
who could be expected to exert race appeal. A third had a wife
and children, a lever for lawyers who would need to play
on sympathy. Viola, of them all, had nothing. She was alone in
the world, a dogged but not vital adjunct to the Communist
Party, and she bore an unfortunate resemblance to Man O' War
in his heyday. At a Party board meeting, it was decided Viola
was expendable. The others, each with his individual propaganda value, were not. For these three the Party secured

lawyers whose rates came high, staged rallies, and went into a frenzy of birthday parties. One week there were six in a row—and no comrade questioned it. Why shouldn't six birthdays occur in a row, especially at a time like this?

By then, there was a new gimmick added. A cake with candles. One giant cake bore a hundred of them, for a woman who couldn't have been more than forty. The privilege of blowing these out one by one was on sale for whatever the comrade wished to bid. The ten-dollar bidders usually began the festivities, and it was all under the direction of a master of ceremonies with a laugh like the hinges of a disused door. It is difficult on any kind of birthday cake to blow out one candle without blowing out others and this made for much gaiety. The ten-dollar blower was assessed an extra five for each one he extinguished by accident. Since Communists are not as a rule very well heeled, the gaiety did not always extend to the blower. But he'd pay up, even baring his teeth in something that may have been a smile. No one could blow for less than a dollar, but no one ever declined. That way lay madness.

There were bazaars as well. For these the wives of lowly Communists were set to work in the kitchen, for the bazaars depended on food booths to a great extent for their revenues. Many of these women were good cooks and, planning beforehand, would fall into acrid discussions on what made the best kind of shortcake or blintzes. Listening to these, I was able sometimes to relax. These were simply housewives, far away from the Kremlin, and for a few minutes the tremors of world conspiracy disappeared. These women were, as a matter of fact, not dangerous as individuals, only as a group. They were Communists because their husbands were Communists. They were Communists because they couldn't imagine what else they were. They didn't know what it was all about and they didn't care. But each of their votes was as valuable as any other vote, and their blintzes were apt to be delicious.

Out of the birthday parties and the bazaars, the Party was able to raise enough for lawyers who could and did stall the cases of the writer, the Korean and the family man. All three are still in Los Angeles, no nearer deportation, so far as I can gather, than when they came to trial. But Viola got the boot. There weren't many things she could do that a trained seal couldn't do, and her rather pathetic loyalty counted for nothing. I saw her off at the bus when she started on the long road back to Liverpool. Her plain, equine face was stupid with incredulity, but she spoke not a word against anyone. She gave her best wishes especially to a comrade who not only had urged she be sluffed off but had said at one of the meetings we held to discuss the cases that she made him nervous—he never knew when she might flare her nostrils and neigh.

Viola was another of the ones who had turned away once and for all from the life she had made, and now had been waved into vacuum. One of the Party saw her later in Liverpool. She was still a Communist, friendless, patient, waiting for deliverance from political exile. It is best she not hold her breath until it comes.

It is a peculiar fact, if any action of Communists can be looked on as peculiar, that these people who deny God yet do not hesitate to utilize religious holidays toward their own ends. They are atheists by fiat—extraordinary phrase: "I order you not to believe in God!"—but at the proper times assemble their own versions of the holy days. Passover, Christmas, Thanksgiving—all come in handy, and the Marxist conception of what they really mean fills the air. So do collection plates. But it is worth your Party reputation to observe the rituals in orthodox fashion. A woman comrade came to our house one evening, breezed in without knock or warning, and saw the children saying prayers. She started to talk fast, but I talked faster. It was a whim of their grandparents, I said, and it was easier to let the youngsters go ahead than to make a scene and create an issue they wouldn't have understood.

This was the woman who on another night had made a grim effort to brainwash Paul, Jr. She was pretty weird, this female, and never more so than on that occasion. In order that there be no doubt she was of the masses, she ate with her elbows on the table, talked with her mouth full, and, when the time came, said delicately: "Where's the can?" She knew better. She could suppress her vulgarity at will. But here was a gal who felt she had to go all the way. She robbed both Paul and me of any appetite. Then after dinner, she started on young Paul.

I was stacking the dishes and didn't hear the first part. When I returned to the living room, she was asking my six-year old son if he understood why Trotsky was a deviationist. This is a gambit guaranteed not to open the floodgates to conversation with a six-year-old. When little Paul had mumbled something indistinguishable, she said: "Well, do you know anything about God? You know He's just a fairy tale, don't you? He's somebody grown-ups made up to scare people. But I can see you don't scare easy. Do you?"

I whisked the boy off to bed, thinking hard, and when I got back I berated Mrs. Elbows for her conduct, though not on maternal grounds. "You're doing a dangerous thing," I pointed out. "Children talk. Half our value to the Party lies in our not being identified with the Party, or anyway not much. I don't want to report you but I don't want it to happen again." Mrs. Elbows crumpled.

But she was only one of her stripe. Vulgarity is a hallmark of the lesser Communists. We were hosts one night to a gathering.

After dinner this time there was a delightful Bohemian touch, quite widely divorced from brandy, cigars and shall-we-join-the-ladies. The gentlemen removed their shoes and put their feet on the coffee table. Maybe Lenin said at one time or another that washing one's socks was a mark of bourgeois degeneracy. If he did, these gentlemen hadn't forgotten his words. We opened every window but not even a cross-draft was effective.

Some later visitors, a week after, were much more "refeened" —a word we have for anyone who retires behind his handkerchief before picking his teeth. They didn't take their shoes off. Well, I hadn't expected them to, since I had no reason to think they were Communists save for the one woman I had known as a girl in Florida. She was the class-conscious one I mentioned in an early chapter. I was to know later that now she was hip-deep in the movement, but our paths hadn't recrossed until then. She was with her husband, a non-Communist who shortly was to divorce her out of a feeling of profound disgust, and two other couples.

The conversation of the group, I abstaining and Paul rather pointedly nasty, which is not usual for him, had mainly to do with literature and the arts, and the conformity of opinion was surprising and a little dull. In most gatherings you can expect a measure of polite disagreement. I imply to their subject matter no overtones of political prejudice but I remember it well enough. In the field of contemporary writing, they held hopes for Norman Mailer and Jean-Paul Sartre, Howard Fast and Mike Gold—diversified talents, to be sure. In films, they revered Mr. Chaplin, the actor; Mr. John Howard Lawson, the writer; and Mr. Biberman, the producer, and his actress wife, a Miss Sondergaard. On another producer, a rising young man, and a prominent actor who also sings (or is it a prominent singer who also acts?), they reserved judgment. They called down maledictions on Mr. Gary Cooper, Mr. Menjou and Miss ZaSu Pitts. They were careful to point out they were speaking in terms of professional merit, nothing else.

I learned from them that night, if they were correct, that five of the Unfriendly Ten, the screen writers who hated to give Congress so much as the time of day, were back in Hollywood functioning as though nothing had ever happened, albeit under names not their own, and that this was done with the connivance of certain major studios. The news seemed to please them. They spoke warmly of three men holding high office in the State of California. On the hostile side, one said he had long had an ambition to take a poke at John Wayne, the actor, on sight. To anyone who knows even roughly the size of John Wayne, this would have been fascinating.

There was about them all the same air of weary, raised-eyebrow "sophistication" I had noted so long ago in my Miami girl friend, and she had lost none of it. When they had gone, Paul stood with his head out the window. "I have to breathe air."

"I didn't like them either."

"It's not liking or not liking. They were Communists, all but that poor guy your friend married. That's enough for me."

"Oh, now, Paul! How do you know?"

"How do I *know?* The same way I know a blind man when I see him. He carries a white cane and—and he's blind. They might as well carry the hammer and sickle on their license plates. Couldn't you see it?"

"I saw the cynicism. But not every cynic's a Communist."

"That's not cynicism. It's half-baked affectation. It's too damn bad punks like that can be dangerous, but they are."

"You mean like half-baked kids with switch-blades?"

"Switch-blades *and* a vicious streak. Don't forget that."

"Well. Maybe you're wrong. Anyway, you're elected to dry the dishes."

He wasn't wrong, at least not far wrong.

Incidentally, one of the women there that night was a lawyer whom I had known well in Miami. We had a blow-up one night and she's refused to talk to me on the phone since. This has been embarrassing, since she is at the time of writing executor of our will. I do not allege she is a Communist.

Hmmm. Here's something that was lost in the shuffle, here in my notes. One word. Spit. It goes back to when I crossed the picket line at the nursery school. There was a small demand afterward that I apologize publicly to my club for the infraction. I did so. No one seemed to care especially one way or the other except a middle-aged woman, a near neighbor of mine, who howled for my expulsion from the Party, denounced me in unprintable terms, and declared that any picket line is a sacred picket line, any strike a good strike. Even for Communism, she was a trifle arbitrary. Her motion was overruled, but from that day forward and until this day, she has spat whenever she sees me. Passing me once in her car, she rolled down the window and let fly to leeward. I dreamed once that by some fantastic sequence of events, we had met in Romanoff's and I am still sorry I woke up before I found out what happened.

Life went on, meetings went on. The woman who had first been my superior in the offices of the Foreign Born Committee and the Civil Rights Congress (now defunct) went to jail for the customary reason and was succeeded by a woman who berated me unceasingly for devoting so much effort to the well-being of my children. She considered my attitude a capitalist aberration and thought it would be better for all children to be brought up in igloos. Plenty of rest and three meals a day, she thought, made pampered dullards of them. One spring, I remember, the fogs became impenetrable so that driving nights was out of the question. But not for Communists. The one time I complained I was read an entire chapter from *Das Kapital*. I think leg-irons would have been preferable.

I cannot forget a dinner given for the cause of embattled North Koreans. I was made ill anyway by the thought of attending; a determining factor in my agreeing to serve the FBI had been the death in Korea of a neighbor's son, one of the first to go. It did not settle my nausea to have my hostess at this dinner roll a chicken leg lovingly between her hands before putting it on my plate. Paul rescued me, saying quickly, "That's mine! Marion doesn't like the legs." I *do* like drumsticks but atop everything else, the woman hadn't washed her hands. It takes a strong stomach sometimes.

One of the sisterhood bragged at meetings of her success in introducing Sunday school tots in the precepts of Communism. She had secured the job of Sunday school teacher by much effort and thought now she was making it pay. I managed to warn various parents of this ploy and our teacher comrade was summarily fired. I doubt that she got far in any event, but I would not underestimate the Communist determination to get them as young as possible.

My cloak and dagger activities seem to me rather pale in comparison to those I have read of, but there were some. There was the time I inveigled a suspected Communist powerhouse to dinner at a fashionable Sunset Strip restaurant and engaged his attention while a "waiter" walked off with his water glass. The waiter was a Federal agent and water glasses take wonderful fingerprints. There were a few tense moments when FBI men were forced to stand behind our bedroom doors until surprise Communist visitors had come and gone.

There was the night I walked away from a meeting without my handbag and hence without my notes, which that night had been copious and far beyond the call of my secretarial duties with the Party. I was half an hour away from the place we had met before·I missed the bag. I'm sorry there are so few Dr. Fu Manchus in real life, but a thing like this can be frightening enough. That bag, lying on a sofa in a living room, could have been opened by anyone and there I would have been. Well, *where* would I have been? I've often wondered. I drove back and retrieved the bag, explaining the importance of transcribing the notes before morning, and that was that.

But I was never able to forget—nor can I forget now—the newspaper photos I saw of a young UCLA student whose dead body (unquestionably he was murdered) was found in the pit of a furnace room beneath a men's dormitory on the campus. Plainly he had died in agony, though medical science never disclosed in detail how. His body was twisted, his face thrown back, his mouth contorted. The pictures came back to me when I met the FBI and, for them, the Party. I would see this body clearly whenever I entered a meeting, whenever I left, now and then while I was making notes of the forbidden kind, masking them behind doodles.

I had talked by then to the mother of a boy who had roomed with the murdered man at Stanford. It was assured he had been a Communist. I later learned that on the day of his murder, he had planned to defect and was going to turn over the information he had to Federal sources. If they would kill once, why not again? If they'd bring death to him, why not to me?

Cuddly thoughts like this precipitated the first erosion of my morale. My nerves began skidding early in 1953 and Paul, deeming my value to the Bureau to be fairly high, took steps to shore me up. The most spectacular of these was to call a radio announcer we both admired, explain the set-up to him, and ask that he, the announcer, aid in rallying my forces. The only catch was that in so doing, Paul had loosed a secret. Understandably, the announcer called the FBI before he did anything else, and the FBI called Paul. They were pleasant but firm. And the ending was happy. I myself realized my reports were being read, that I *was* doing some good, and I snapped back again.

I'm glad I did. I think now of things I was able to pass on. I remember when bail had to be raised in the amount of $20,000 for each of twelve Communist defendants in a deportation hassle—a staggering amount of money—and the purchase of Government E Bonds was discussed. (Communists thought nothing of using United States interest rates to fight the United States.) Someone spoke of a windfall when the bonds should fall due, and a leading comrade said in my presence: "Fall due! You're thinking very small. When these bonds are due, we'll be running the country and we won't be using E Bonds for anything but wallpaper."

I remember the words of the Communist who was a candidate for high public office, a lawyer, an Irishman loaded to the gunwales with careless bravado.

He spoke that night of Communist members who waited in jails: "These are the real heroes, the advance guard of a world-wide movement which in due time will wipe out the existing order!" Clear enough?

And naturally I remember Washington in the fall of 1955 and my testimony that was to be the summation of the years and the tears and the pain. And what came after, I remember that.

It doesn't matter. I'd do it all again, and again after that, if need be.

Washington was pleasant that autumn. I mean by that, the weather was. My notes are a shambles now but I remember without referring to them that the gentleman who cross-examined me was not pleasant at all. I am not surprised at that. I am only surprised that I *don't* remember what he looked like. Frankenstein's monster, I suppose.

14

Yesterday

IT WAS APRIL OF 1955 WHEN TWO WASHINGTON AT-
torneys called on me in Los Angeles with a request that would
seem on the surface anti-climactic but was in fact the fore-
runner of what was to me a critical decision. They wished me
to testify before the Subversive Activities Control Board to
what I had learned in my years of counter-espionage. It was
not to be a closed hearing.

The purpose had in essence a limited objective: to establish
a link between the Los Angeles Committee for Protection
of Foreign Born and the national committee bearing the same
name. One would suppose a five-year old child would assume
the connection but the letter of the law is, fortunately for us
all, considerably more complex and finicky than a five-year old
child. The national committee—the five-year old child *is* permitted this deduction—had already been cited as a Communist front. That, of course, was what all the shooting was about,
to begin with.

I have used "anti-climactic" here as a throwaway word, yet
in a sense the lawyers' visit *was* anti-climactic and my decision
to cooperate with the Board even more so.

Why now all the months of fear that the Communists would discover me for what I was, the times of frenzy, the tears, the hysteria and the nightmares? What a waste of abject terror! Now I was going to turn my cards up anyway, in full view of every one of them.

It is one thing to be decorated as a successful spy and publicly cited for the accomplishment when you are back with your own army, safe within the cordon of your friends, the enemy routed. It is quite another to reveal what you have done while still surrounded by the enemy camp.

How many times had I climbed stairs to Party meetings choked with apprehension that they awaited me with clubs, that they had discovered all? What of the night I had run the red lights in panic, had had the drink I was so afraid contained poison, had gagged with fright that my notes had been examined, had succumbed to nausea when my Communist superiors had called me on the carpet?

I might as well have saved myself the trouble. If I had known I was going to offer myself up to them, come what might, I might have managed the whole business with the calm of fatalistic resignation. I wouldn't have lost the weight I did, perhaps. I wouldn't have missed the meals. I would, in sum, have enjoyed all the compensatory comforts of martyrdom.

On the other hand, I might have pulled out of the affair before I had begun, and that wouldn't have done at all!

But now, when I thought it was all over, I was handed the ultimate decision. The lurking dread lurked no longer. It had come right out in the open, wearing across its breast a ribbon labeled PATRIOTISM. The chances of disclosure had been the root of all my fears. Now disclosure was a committed course of action—and one not to be withdrawn. When I said yes to the Washington lawyers, I said it without reservation.

It's funny how the mind will accept finality when all along it has boggled and jittered at the threat of finality. When I made my commitment, my only immediate feeling was regret over the agonies of foreboding I had undergone for nothing, since now I was to dive into the soup anyway. The diver in physical fact, the one who dawdles endlessly on the high platform, must have the same fractional relief when finally he tilts his weight irrevocably over the edge. Uncertainty and apprehension are the real devils, and making up your mind brings its own anaesthesia. I don't necessarily mean by this that "nothing's as bad as you think it will be." That particular saw has to me the sinister overtone of so many pat declarations, a suggestion of glibness substituted for thought, optimism for reality. The high diver may feel relief one moment and break his neck the next. But the relief of commitment is genuine.

I don't have to say that in my own case the worst of my forebodings did not materialize. For example, I'm still alive. Lesser forebodings did come about as expected but by the same token, I had written them off in advance. The sharpest hurts, as I've said in the beginning, were from sources and for reasons I'd never anticipated.

When I gave my word to the lawyers, I was not long recuperative from my ulcer attack; and at that, the hospital had released me with some misgivings. Now naturally I awaited a resumption of pain. None came. The duodenum behaved like a lamb. There were months to go before Washington and the formal unveiling of my villainy, but they were unexpectedly pacific months. I was relaxed, and ate well and slept well and did all the other things the doctor ordered. This was not the ulcer doctor, this was the obstetrician. Bobby was en route.

I don't say or imply that Paul and I were in a state of elation. The peace of acceptance was there but roiled by the knowledge that the danger at last was manifest. Our assurances to one another they "they" could now do their damnedest did not ring true, because their damnedest would have involved the children. In conversation, I had to admit to Paul that I'd bitten off more than I ever meant to chew and that, come to think of it, I hadn't bitten it off, it had been stuffed into my mouth.

"You can spit it out again."

"You know I'm fooling. No, I'm not. It *was* stuffed into my mouth. But I'm glad it has been. I'm glad to know I'm going all the way."

"You may think," he said, "that what you've done for the FBI is enough. I wouldn't really blame you."

"Nothing's enough."

He laughed. "Bravo! Now I think I've married Joan of Arc."

"No. I don't mean to sound square. But—you know."

"Sure I know. What do you think I've been doing, whittling?"

"You're not going before the Justice Department like I am."

"No, but I would. If they wanted me. Besides I'll be in it as deep as you once it gets out."

"Of course you will, honey. I was kidding." I was, too. But Paul wasn't. He wasn't kidding. Paul envied me this last phase of my job, come to me at a time when the FBI had bowed to my ulcers and released me and even the Party had had to confess I could no longer be of any use to them. Paul would have shinnied up a Congressman's back to get his ear, and called a press conference while he was shinnying. Where Communists are concerned, Paul revels in the climate of trouble. Under Red attack he eats six meals a day and sleeps like a child. I could wish I were like that. Instead:

"I'm worried sick about the children."

His face lost the gay, defiant lines. "So am I. But we mustn't.

That would be giving them a little victory, a tiny one. We can't give them any victories at all."

"We could move away from here. After the hearing, I mean. Go somewhere and change our names."

He stood, walked to the kitchen, and walked back again. "We're going nowhere. They'll never do that to us. If they can, if they make us run, then we've erected a police state of our own and we'll have to live in it as long as we do live. I'll die before the children are harmed. You know that. I'm not hamming, I'm just telling you a fact. I don't have the guns just for effect. But we're not going anywhere, not now or ever. That would be a death in itself."

"You don't really think they'll do us harm anyway, do you? That *is* your honest opinion?"

"That's my honest opinion. They're too disciplined and cagey, the rank and file. At least the big shots are too cagey. I'm just afraid of the looneys, the cranks."

"Well—aren't they all?"

"Don't get started on that. It's a deeper lunacy. They'd wipe out a nation if they needed to but not even swat a hornet if it were only a question of getting even. Killing for vindictiveness alone is wasteful and it does entail risk. They *do* have that kind of reasoning. Once you've testified, the damage is done, so what could they gain? And if anything did happen to you after that, they'd be first on the suspect list and don't think they don't know it."

"Yes, but the children."

"Same thing."

"It all sounds like the middle chapters of a dull mystery story." Suddenly I felt rocky. "I'm going to lie down."

"All right. See if the kids are asleep."

"Oh, they're asleep. Sit on the front steps with your pistols and watch for the cranks." I tried to smile but couldn't.

"You haven't testified yet."

"No, but I'm going to."

Washington in early October of that year both was and wasn't the city I had worked in during the war. Downtown it was bigger and harder and glossier than then; visionaries from the North, I guessed, had brushed aside the Mason-Dixon line and imposed their own brand of architecture on office building. But out on the periphery the indolent beauties of tradition were the same as ever. I'm told some of the residences in Georgetown go back two hundred years. If it is so, they built lovely homes then. Geometrically, of course, everything was the same; the circles each the hub of an area, the streets the spokes of the wheel. There is none of the numerical precision of New York. I got lost, naturally. It is said that if one can find his way around Los Angeles, he's equal to anything, including the Matto Grosso country of Brazil. This may be, but Washington is a worthy foe.

The gentleman handling this stage of the prosecution for the Government met my plane, deposited me at my hotel and left me to the cool mercies of being a stranger. I hoped, at any rate, that I was a stranger. No Communist, so far as I was aware, knew anything of my presence there, let alone the reason for it. But on that first Sunday I went out three times and each time the same man was walking away from my door, always with an air of having a pressing destination. When I came back the third time, I had difficulty with my key, as though someone had been tampering with the lock. Not long afterward I was moved to another hotel.

Eric Ambler, the skilled British writer of international hanky-panky, would make more out of this than I can. But then again, there are certain marvelous advantages to dealing in fiction. I was moved to another hotel, nothing happened, and that was that.

Well, I won't say "nothing." I did spend five days on the stand telling all I knew.

Some people are unbearably fascinated by literal transcript, the Q. and the A., and especially literal transcript of courtroom or committee proceedings. I am not, and I hope that you're not either. Of my own testimony, I can say only that it was either extraneous to this book, overlapping material already dealt with, or simply dull. If you feel you must have it, however, I understand it is obtainable for three hundred and something dollars, prepaid, Washington, D. C. That is, copies of it are. I'd suggest you skip it, as I'm going to.

"My" lawyer, the Government attorney conducting our side of the hearing, led me through two and a half days of testimony gently as one would lead a child through a bramble thicket. In cross-examination the attorney for the other side had more the attitude of wanting to kick the little dear into a bear trap. This man, whom I learned to detest in no time, may have been an excellent lawyer but no cross-examiner on earth can shake absolute unadorned truth, which my answers were from first to last.

The whole thing, all the hours and days, came to this: the Government—"we"—was intent on establishing that the Los Angeles Committee for Protection of Foreign Born was part of the national committee bearing the same name. For the years before, there had been one link between the two and only one: I. By that I mean, one flesh-and-blood link. I was the Los Angeles committee's delegate to the gatherings of the Communist Party and vice versa. No other human strip of adhesive tape could so testify. Important? I'll fall back again on my old figure of speech —if one loses the smallest part of a jigsaw puzzle, then the puzzle is never finished. One may assume that the lost part fits but assumptions are not so strong under the law. Now the adhesive factors shrank even further: if, it seemed, the defense attorney failed to shake me loose from my sequence on the smallest details, the stickum became useless and unreliable. I could only pray I would not fail, that I would remember truly that this or that interorganization memo was on yellow paper, not pink. (The opposing lawyer tried, I think seven times once to make me say it was pink.) I believe I survived.

But I barely survived a more mundane crisis. It had nothing, or anyway little, to do with mental confusion. After a long time on the stand, I had simply and most purely to go to the powder room. The defense, by not pausing, was browbeating an *enceinte* lady. May a witness interrupt the grandeur of the law for so niggling an inconvenience? I did. Anyway, what's niggling about it?

The defense, the American Committee for Protection of Foreign Born, appeared in the person of its head official, a man now dead. I had met him several times in Los Angeles and knew him casually. But no words passed between us at this reunion, nothing but cold stares.

There was an audible gasp from spectators when my name was called by the prosecution and, after a few minutes, one of them made a hurried exit from the press section. I was told later the man who hustled out represented Tass, the Soviet news agency. It is my presumption that he telephoned his comrades in Los Angeles with the tidings. In any event, they were waiting for me.

I flew back to Los Angeles the following week. Paul, who had

stayed behind with the children, had ready for me a clipping
from the *Daily People's World*, a strange little paper that does
not adore me to this day. Here is what it said:

"Los Angeles, Oct. 5—Mrs. Marian *(sic)* Miller, 1007 Esther
Ave., West Los Angeles, was revealed today as having been an
FBI stoolpigeon in the ranks of the Los Angeles Committee for
Protection of Foreign Born.

"The foreign born committee announced that Mrs. Miller had
appeared as a government witness Tuesday before the Subversive Activities Control Board in Washington.

"During her brief testimony she said she had joined the Los
Angeles Committee at a Founding conference in 1950. She
took notes of the proceedings at the conference, and later, she
testified, gave them to her husband, Paul Miller, who turned
them over to the FBI.

"Purpose of her testimony, the government explained, was to
attempt to link the Los Angeles committee with the much older
established National Committee for Protection of Foreign Born
and thus brand the Los Angeles organization 'subversive' by
virtue of association.

"Contention of the Los Angeles committee is that it was
established and has operated at all times as an independent
organization, having only fraternal association with the national committee.

"Local committee spokesmen said that Mrs. Miller had remained an active member of the local committee until about a
year ago. At that time she became suspected of being an agent
after many persons had reported her avidity for note-taking at
meetings. She claimed she suffered a nervous breakdown at
the time. She is the mother of two small children.

"When the SACB hearings recessed Tuesday, Mrs. Miller
was excused temporarily, but instructed to return for cross-
examination by attorneys for the foreign born committee early
next week."

Appearing in the newspaper as it did, this account seemed to
me admirably restrained. My first name was misspelled, my
address incorrect and the use of the word "stoolpigeon" perhaps
not consistent with the canons of objective journalism, but I
was not accused of poisoning dogs or contemplating matricide.
I *was* upset by the reference to my two children, which struck
me as being oddly out of context with the whole, but I set my
alarm down to emotional strain. My third child, Bobby, was
about ready to join the human race.

Paul then presented me with the capper. This was the open
letter from the local committee. I have already mentioned it.
It was handicapped by none of the constraints imposed on
press distribution. It had been mailed or delivered to hundreds
on hundreds of my friends, my neighbors, members of clubs I
had belonged to or still did, strangers both interested and otherwise. I reproduce it here as a fair sample of the old Communist
manner, the one so effectively muffled nowadays, *and* as a
document that affected my life adversely for months and even
years to come. One would think today, reading it, that its very
blatancy would indicate the true source and render it innocuous
as an attacking weapon. But one would be wrong.

"Dear Neighbor" was its salutation. "*Informers* (italics and
capital letters are the letter's) are hated by all fair-minded
people in the United States, as they have been throughout the
history of mankind. When the rights and freedoms of the
people were under attack during Thomas Jefferson's day, with
the government encouraging the use of informers to enforce the
Alien and Sedition Laws, Edward Livingstone told Congress:
"'The country will swarm with informers, spies, and all the
odious reptile tribe that breed in the sunshine of despotic
power! The hours of the most unsuspected confidence, the

intimacies of friendship, or the recess of domestic retirement afford no security.'

"MARION MILLER IS A MEMBER OF SUCH A 'REPTILE TRIBE'!! She lives with her husband, Paul Miller, at 10716 Esther Avenue, West Los Angeles.

"During the week of October 3rd, *Marion Miller* testified before a government board, admitting that ever since 1950 she had been employed as a spy by the F.B.I. She joined a local group raising funds to maintain a home for the aged, a nursery school, a synagogue, various women's organizations, and a committee which defends the rights of foreign-born citizens and residents of the United States—all *for the admitted purpose of taking minutes* of meetings, *stealing letters and other records* from the files, *recording the names* of persons attending meetings and what they had to say, AND TURNING ALL INFORMATION OVER TO THE F.B.I. FOR *DISTORTION* TO ACHIEVE INTIMIDATION."

"Perhaps, as a neighbor, Marion Miller is known to you. Perhaps, like many of her *former friends* and neighbors, you accepted her as a devoted and sincere person who was honest in her defense of under-privileged and persecuted persons, and in her work in worthy causes.

"IT IS BITTER FOR A FAIR-MINDED AMERICAN WITH PRIDE IN OUR DEMOCRATIC TRADITIONS, TO THINK THAT THESE VERY QUALITIES OF SEEMING SINCERITY AND DEVOTION TO WORTHY CAUSES WERE EXPLOITED BY THE F.B.I.—CORRUPTED INTO THEIR OPPOSITE: *dishonesty . . . theft . . . invasions of privacy . . . spying on everyone with whom MARION MILLER came into contact!*

"This is an evil and immoral use of government power! A recent editorial in the New York TIMES stated:

" 'The process of informing is a dirty business and one that does not become well a free society. It implies accusation without proof, defamation without responsibility . . . *The INFORMER smacks of the police-state;* and we think that most Americans instinctively shrink from this use. It is reasonable to suppose that the professional, paid informers feel the necessity of *continuing to produce* if they are not to give up their lucrative occupations . . .'

"IS IT NOT CONTEMPTIBLE OF *Marion Miller,* daughter of immigrant parents, to lend herself to unscrupulous spying and theft of records from an organization defending 130 victims of the 'racist and discriminatory' Walter McCarran Immigration and Nationality Law, which every democratic organization in the country has condemned. She sold her soul for a few pieces of silver!

"Please bring this leaflet to the attention of your parents or social group,—your union, your church or synagogue, as a lesson in infamy flowing out of these 'reptile-breeding' times when free speech is suppressed by government agencies, and decent human qualities are distorted by a police body such as the F.B.I."

The signature said that the leaflet was "issued as a public service" by the L.A. Committee for Protection of Foreign Born and that additional copies could be procured from the committee's address, 326 West 3rd Street, Room 318, Los Angeles 13, California. Down the left side of the prose, if such it was, were three line-drawings, captioned from top to bottom "The Informer" (a woman—me, I suppose—behaving in sneaky fashion), "The Victim" (impoverished soul pointing sadly to Statue of Liberty), and "Deported" (ship sailing past Statue of Liberty, which either is wearing a sequin dress or is pickled with holes, like Swiss cheese).

I may not be the person to describe the document as inflammatory, since it is directed mainly at me and only incidentally at the methods of United States democracy. But I certainly am the one to attest that it did inflame.

It inflamed many and various persons, uniformly anonymous,

who wrote us the letters that jammed our mailbox. I'll present a few of these in a minute. It inflamed those of my clubs to which I still belonged. The ones that had not dropped me for being a suspected Communist now dropped me for being a suspected—an accused—thief, spy and meddler. It inflamed the person who shot at me and mine. The tinkle of glass came first, then the whine of a bullet's flight, the rifle crack last of all. Wonderment, the mad and uncoordinated dashings about, shock, terror, police and newsmen all followed in something like that order. It inflamed the ones among Paul's customers who dropped him as their poster artist, and some of these it did not inflame suffered an emasculation of the fighting heart. They sneaked to Paul in his studio after dark, explaining apologetically they couldn't afford to be seen coming or going.

As I have written in the beginning, most of the neighbors turned on us, many of our erstwhile friends. For the children, innocent and not understanding, the world became terribly cruel. Sometimes little boys and girls take pleasure in cutting one out of the pack and attacking him or her—this time, him *and* her. Paul, Jr., and Betsy were, and they are, sensitive and friendly. They are not loudly gregarious but they like and they want to be liked. Their persecution by their playmates, who usually were just carrying out a mandate of their parents, was senseless.

But who was to know that? The leaflet, if you will note back, had accused me of spy actions sweepingly, stated I had spied on every group I had joined. And if the groups as a whole did not believe it, some members at least behaved as though they did.

The obscene and threatening propagators of the phone calls we received—these surely were inflamed. Many were Communists, yes, but not all. We were able at times to recognize the voices, and they seemed about evenly divided between the two camps.

We were able, too, to recognize the handwriting on some of the delightful letters. This one, for example, we recognized:

"I have been meaning to write you (since the testimony). You will now be sending us anti-Communist propaganda, I'm sure. Just exactly what are you trying to accomplish?

"Do you think that anything written by you, about you or for you could possibly interest me? Both of you are degenerates—both of you have sick minds—both of you are the most hated type of person in history—the *stool pigeon*, the informer, the liar!

"You have disgraced our American heritage and your anti-Communist ravings do not insure your Americanism. It reminds me of the Nazi way of life, the same way of life that led to the extinction of millions of Jews. The fact that *you* are Jews, that you are *informer Jews*, is a disgrace to our people. The most despised person in Jewish history is the informer.

"Can you sleep at night? I wonder how you can stop from thinking about the families that have been tortured by your so-called 'testimony'. Can't you get a job as a typist or a salesperson? Or are you only fit for spying? Why has it been your decision to become professional stoolies? Why is it necessary for you to mind other people's business?

"The issue of Communists destroying our country is ridiculous and you know it. There are only a handful. So why—ask yourself, why are you spending your lives hounding people, making everyone who is decent *hate* you and your kind?"

The writer is a woman and, to the best of my knowledge, not a Communist.

This one's a Communist but she does address me as Darling

Marion and signs herself "A Friend". I should cultivate my enemies. The letter was written, as you see, not too long ago:

"Are you going to help Ike and Dick entertain Nikita? Bring all those citations and gifts (for FBI work: MM), also the nice things you bought with the blood money you received. *Show all this to Nikita!*

"I feel sorry for your poor children. Live a long time if you have to but move away from here. I can't wait!"

She was confused that day. Her letters just after I got back from Washington were more lucid and explicit and used four-letter words that always were spelled correctly. So were the five-, six-, and seven-letter words.

A third . . . Oh, let's not. We have bales of these letters, Paul and I, and would use them for a more utilitarian purpose than we do except that logs burn so much longer. They are not secrets, but an exasperating incoherency marks most of them so that they contribute nothing to the sum total of human knowledge, let alone the Communist apologia. If Communists must answer charges of conspiracy by advocating that the accuser turn blue and drop dead, then Communism intellectually is in desperate straits. (Would that that were the case. As I've pointed out, it isn't.) If friends of anti-Communists believe the first Communist counter-attack they hear and therewith turn on the anti-Communist, then their friendship would seem a bit leaky.

I offer one more piece of correspondence, but only because I have a reason for doing so. It is a copy of a letter directed not to us but to a mailing list at random, in the manner of the broadside already reprinted. It was mailed in July of 1959 and refers to the wearisome charge that Paul and I were paid for counter-espionage by the United States Government. The writer is a prominent woman Communist who at that time was out of jail. She speaks specifically of an article in a Red paper reiterating the old lie.

"We wish to call your attention to the enclosed article, which gives some data concerning the informer, Marion Miller. She is, according to the article, nothing but a *paid* informer who regarded spying as an avocation of some sort. Mrs. Miller spied on our organization (the Foreign Born Committee: MM), which defends noncitizens in deportation matters, and with other organizations fights the Walter-McCarran Law.

"Mrs. Miller spied on other organizations *for a price*. In all her appearances she never mentioned the fact that she was getting paid for her sordid work. She rather posed as a self-sacrificing super-patriot, and it is for this reason that we are sending you the enclosed clipping . . ." The rest concerns something else.

I have been advised by very well-meaning friends that to deny the Red allegation that I was paid for spying by the FBI or some other U.S. agency would be to dignify the report. Maybe so. Let it be dignified nonetheless. Paul and I, together or separately, never profited for or from the years we practiced espionage for the FBI. Now, years later, organizations that wish to pay us for appearances as speakers in the cause of anti-Communism do so. If they're not able to, we frequently speak anyway, where possible. That's it; not more, not less.

The rest of this chapter is to some extent a reprise of the first. The convulsive Communist rage that I had been a spy, an informer and finally a deponent for the people before a body of the Government—this we knew would happen. We just didn't know how. We did not anticipate the leaflet but for no better reason than that there was no way of knowing *what* to anticipate. We were perhaps unduly shocked by its effectiveness but consoled ourselves by reminding one another there had been no refutation as yet, by us or anyone else in a position to know the facts. The FBI's position re its counterspies is (because it has to be) the less said, the better. No additional help was going to come from that source. Still, it seemed to us, someone besides the Communists would have to say something. My years of work and my culminating testimony continued to be an unknown quantity to all but a select few—and most of these selected by the Communists.

That was Paul's cue. As I've said, he parlayed the Miller story from the neighborhood papers up through the dailies and from them to *This Is Your Life*. By the classic rule of thumb, that should have been the happy ending. We didn't want a ticker-tape parade, God knows, but we did want vindication. What we got was what I can call at best a mixed jury. The hail of abuse from non-Communists went right on, although in a somewhat different tone. The Communists had got there fustest and the indent of their lying thrust on a virgin surface would not disappear. In the minds of hundreds, of thousands, I was still a busybody who rummaged through other people's filing cabinets, any filing cabinets I could get my hands on. Those who never saw the follow-up stories were convinced of this, and those who seldom read anything but accept hearsay as probable truth weren't at all certain I hadn't been a Communist from the first—"And you can bet your bottom nickel she still is, I don't care *what* the papers say. Edie heard from whatzername down at the market that this is all a cover-up, and you know Edie's got to know what she's talking about before she'll say it!"

There were conservatives among our one-time friends who shied from the publicity, recoiling that the memoirs of an exhibitionist had impinged on the smugness of their cosy obscurity. The Jews among these spoke in some cases out of caution, and I felt desperately sorry for them, and I always will. Was it some atavism? Did they still identify with Berlin in the 1930's, even though they had never lived there? Was it a feeling if they were quiet as mice, the Gentile overlords might forget them and leave them alone? Dear God, how many American Gentiles joined American Jews in death to stamp out the Third Reich?

The papers had the Miller story right, and all of it in substance: anti-Communist espionage, the years and the fears, the testimony, the Reds lashing back, the ostracism as a result. Ralph Edwards' program was an emotional paean of praise, encouraged by J. Edgar Hoover personally. But we did not walk off into the sunset hand in hand, Paul and I, while the house lights came up and the popcorn venders snapped to attention in the lobby. We groped on, dazed in our personal darkness. What had we done? Why were the voices of gratitude, simple commendation or just friendliness so small and indistinct? Where was our America, so tough and brave, so wonderfully go-to-hell in the way it faced its enemies?

We found out. It was right where it's always been. A little time, that was all it needed. We'll never be out of the woods, not entirely. The years go on and the letters and calls never quite abate. They've found their little level and it doesn't go down, but it doesn't go up either. Besides, we don't care. We've found something better than being in the clear (frankly, it looks lonely out there.) We're still in the woods, yes, but a part of the woods we love. We've found our America all over again and we like to think it's found us. The friends we truly valued have come back. We make new ones every day. Our work goes on through the lectures—that is the blessing. It wouldn't have been enough to rest on our oars. No one can do that now because the enemy never slows its beat. Khrushchev is a ruthless coxswain, his crew more bitterly determined with every stroke.

In the whole world pattern, Paul and I are tiny—so small you can barely see us with a microscope. But Americans do listen to what we have heard and seen, and to what we think can be done, so that some day . . .

So it has been worth while; very, very much so. Now I suppose we might look back and say, well, that's over. But how? The past is over, yes. The future is unknowable. But the present —that is always with us.

15

Today

SPRING CAME TO ESTHER AVENUE EARLY THIS YEAR.
As I write this, there is none of the April mist we are so accustomed to. The jacaranda is coming to bloom, and a small, busy bird is building her nest in the hedge out back. Paul is hard at it in the studio; business has come back all the way and then some. Paul, Jr., and Betsy have left for school. We try not to worry about them now. The police patrol car drives by slowly at the time they leave and when they come home, but this may be merely that that's how its route works out. The weather and the morning are tranquil to the point of being soporific. An overdose of Miltown might produce the same effect.

The paper is beside me. It is bubbling over yesterday's temperature having been a record 91, and how Los Angeles is growing at the rate of so many hundred persons daily. Khrushchev is back in Moscow mad as a wet rooster. He has told Pravda that De Gaulle alone met his approval at the "Summit" that barely got as far as the foothills. It is so hard to see how a man like De Gaulle, with his proud lock on national sovereignty, would come to agreements with Khrushchev, to whom any sovereignty other than Soviet is an affront. But if Krushchev says he did, all right.

In Geneva, the Russians seem to be agreeing that some form of mutual atom bomb inspection might be okay, provided this and provided that—and how about Francis Powers? The Supreme Court has upheld the conviction of a Soviet spy but only by five to four; we seem to have searched his room without asking him if he minded, which is not protocol. The warrant wasn't in order or something. Soviet police slaughtered a hundred rioters in one of their more obscure republics, it says here. That is an internal matter. The Negro race is at long last flexing its muscles in the continent of Africa; the brushfire has extended down now to South Africa where the whites appear to think apartheid is the answer. The situation is very ugly.

News from Red China, filtered through Hong Kong and flanking Asian countries, is not clear at all. Some of our friends consider the "agrarian revolution" there a success. Two of them, however, notably do not; George Lim and Jo Ho. They are Chinese, partners in a distinguished Cantonese restaurant here called the Kowloon. They got out ahead of the agrarians but their channels of information are, they say, beyond question. And beyond question, Red China is a charnel house.

Fidel Castro's government in Cuba is still shooting people. It is impossible to divine Mr. Castro's politics but lately he quacks like a duck. The pundits I trust most on these questions have been saying that if Castro is not a Red, the Reds nonetheless have a hook in his nose. I cannot forget that one could almost skip a flat rock across the water from my Miami to Havana, Miami being an integral part of the United States whatever the unlikely quality of its winter atmosphere. Admiral Stump, who ran our on-the-spot diplomacy in the Pacific

from 1953 to 1958, was in our town, it says here. He told report-
ers World War III has begun.

There's nothing in the paper about two lectures of the
evening before. Paul and I split the billing on one of them,
the other was by a screenwriter who took the Fifth Amendment. I am allowed to mention him by name if I say only that.
I may not mention his name if I say he's a Communist. Who
needs his name? He's a Communist.

It happens all three of us spoke before student audiences.
By phone today I have been told he got the elite of the
undergraduate left wing. That's all right—we don't exactly
mow the left wing elite down in any event. This man, this
Communist, can rely on good support from some of the faculty
of the giant university the students represented. The instructor
or professor tells his classes casually before the end of the
period that this man is going to speak at such-and-such a hall
and that they might find him stimulating. It's a nice plug,
arranged with the screenwriter in advance. In fact, the faculty
of *that* university is being looked into this minute, and with
great care. At any rate, a good share of the students troop in
to hear the speaker, who tells them at the close of his address
that, by the way, a friend of his is having a few people in for
a late snack and those who wish to join him are included in the
invitation. The friend is a powerful figure in entertainment,
capable of giving employment to young people he fancies. He's
a good Communist, too, by which is meant an obedient Communist.

Quite a number of the young people not only are of the left
but also crave entree to Hollywood. Eagerly they go to the
friend's house, are baited with half-promises, and washed a
little behind the lobes of the brain. The great university has

been executing this maneuver for a long time. More accurately, certain members of its faculty have, using the university as a front. This makes the school one of the most formidable Communist dupes in the country. It would be nice if its Regents would snap out of their daze and take counter-action. They don't, in most cases because they are more afraid of the word "reactionary" than any other word, unless it be "witch-hunt" or "Red-baiter." Fear and dislike of these three words are another part of planned Communist appeal to liberal snobbery. It's brainwashing of a really subtle kind.

Paul and I spoke before two hundred or so postgraduates in one of the halls on the campus. That's about our average audience and lets us reach roughly two thousand minds in any given month. We have no fear now of leaving the children behind. There is the sitter, and certain other arrangements that always are made beforehand.

We told—Paul first, I second—of what we had done, what we had seen and heard, and sounded the klaxon of alarm. I don't know what more documentation we could offer than the documentation we do. After we had talked, there was, as there always is, a seminar with those present. They may ask what they like.

We do not invite debate because we object to providing a platform for those in the enemy camp—and a platform is just what they will make of it if given a little leeway—but no questions are barred. The questions aren't always easy, especially those motivated by hostility, and it can even be we are sometimes at a semantic disadvantage. The formulae of science can often get off the ground faster than the affirmations of faith, and carry the day by pyrotechnics. Clarence Darrow— here goes an unfortunate figure of speech—made a monkey out of William Jennings Bryan at the Scopes trial in the 1920's, as a proponent of the theory of evolution. But when you know things to be so, you cannot easily be shaken.

We had one of the militant challengers with us that night. He may have been Communist-planted, he may have had honest intellectual doubts. After a number of polite and relevant queries, he rose and asked me whether it was not true, nobility of purpose aside, that I had stolen from Communist files. When angry I can now think fairly fast on my feet, though Paul is better at it.

"Were you in Korea?" I asked the questioner. He was, I would have judged, in his mid-thirties.

"Yes. That doesn't answer . . ."

"Did you kill any of the enemy?"

"I'm not sure. I think so. What has that to do . . .?"

"Were you then executed for murder?"

"Of course not."

"Of course not. Killing is part of the rules of war. No. To answer your question—I never stole."

"But you're talking of the moral viewpoint."

"What other viewpoint is there?"

Paul stepped in. He said to the questioner: "There was a big league umpire who was asked if he'd ever made a wrong call, a wrong decision. He said, 'Never in my heart.' That answers your question."

I thought we'd won a little victory. The questioner tried another part of the perimeter. By now we know pretty well where they're going to lunge. "Did you approve of Joe McCarthy?"

"Yes." Paul and I have few misgivings about the late Senator McCarthy. We are his admirers. We know it's a controversial point of view and we know there are a lot of fine non-Communists who had no use for him. I can only repeat, we admire Senator McCarthy.

"You don't think he did terrible harm to many innocent people?"

Paul: "Name one."

Our man had been waiting for this. "George Catlett Marshall."

A few weeks before, Paul or I would have replied that McCarthy did not hurt General Marshall, that he was too big a man to be hurt. But it was a shifty answer; it would have offended a logician, and we knew it. Senator McCarthy had come so close to saying General Marshall was a traitor that he might as well have said it.

"Joe McCarthy," said Paul, "was not a perfect man. He made mistakes. That was one. But show me a man who hasn't made mistakes and I'll show you one who's lived all his life in a hermetically sealed room. Marshall honestly thought the Chinese Communists were well-meaning and not a threat. It was a costly error. He may not even have been sure they were Communists."

"But that didn't make him a traitor."

"No, it didn't. Mr. McCarthy went overboard. We admit it. But he was fighting the Communists, remember, and he did till he died. Any man can lose his temper fighting the Communists."

"But you did like McCarthy?" The questioner wasn't going to let go of it.

"We have a few reservations. But the question isn't what *I* thought of McCarthy, it's what the Communists thought of him. What *did* the Communists think of him?" Dear Paul. He believes in a good offense.

"Are you asking *me*?"

"Yes. Can't you answer?"

"Well—undoubtedly they hated him. You're apt to hate anyone who hates *you*. May I ask now what you think the Communist danger is?"

My turn. "You couldn't have been listening to us very hard. It's the danger of despotism, the end of freedom in a country whose reason for living is freedom. It would be concentrated power in the hands of amoral adventurers. They talk of collectivism when all they mean is power. They're out and they want to be in. It's not as simple as that but that's one of the corner stones. And when they're in, you're out." Or are you? Watch it, Marion.

Paul said: You've mentioned the people Joe McCarthy criticized. Have you ever made a study of the people who criticized Joe McCarthy?"

"Lot of good people there."

"Maybe so. What I really meant was, look into their criticisms some time. See how much truth there was in them. They spent four-fifths of their time talking through their hat."

"How about the other fifth?"

"I don't know about you, but I thank God for the other fifth. A right to his opinion is what makes a guy lucky to be living in a country like this. Be sure to tell me next time a Russian gets up in the Praesidium in Moscow and moves to censure Khrushchev, boot him out if he can. I'll want to know what happened."

I'm going to leave this exchange here, but not necessarily to give Paul and me the last word. Among the crashing bores of the world are the narrators who invariably leave the other person crushed and at a loss for words and walk off with garlands twined in their hair. You must have heard them, the paralyzing end of their tale, "And I said to him, 'Listen, you fat slob, you can take your job and dunk it in your coffee!' And out I walked! And you know what he did? Sat there and never said another word—not a *word!* He knew I was right, see?" Well, hurray for our side!

Our questioner that night was not crushed, he had a lot more to say, and he may have ended up with a draw decision. But actually he didn't because he had the old fatal weaknesses that have to beat "them" in the end—he had no affirmations. They can snipe at our safeguards, as Ernest did, perform their negative word-tricks, roll in the sound of their own voice. But in the end they have nothing to say.

Just let no one think that's going to stop them from saying it.

We have much brighter memories. There was the Negro spectator one night who waited for us as we left another hall. He had waited just outside the door, attentive. He thanked us for our words and told us of how the Communists had spent weeks befriending him and his family in an effort to reach him because he was a strong figure in a predominantly Negro political ward. They expended terrific effort and a good deal of money on entertainment. They took him to one place they knew would not serve him and embarrassed him cruelly by making an issue of his being refused admittance.

"There was no need for it," he said. "Communists are fools. They'll never get the Negro people." I thought of "Carl."

"A few of us," he went on, "a few of us they'll get. They make a big to-do about our grievances. What's the use to chew over the grievances when you could use the energy trying to right them. Legislation'll do it some day. Not today, not tomorrow. It's going to take time. These fools, they want their revolution. They're not going to get it. One of them said to me all about how you people, he called you capitalists, all about how you go around talking about equal rights and then say to each other, 'Would you want your sister to marry a Negro?'

"Well, probably you wouldn't, not the way things are today. I wouldn't want my sister to marry one of you either. There's the children to think of, the whole society structure the way it is. Like I say, it won't be forever like this, but you try to change it overnight, you're asking for worse trouble than you've got, than all of us got. I tell you, they're fools, them and their revolution."

"They're a lot worse than fools," said Paul.

"Yes, a lot worse. But they're fools to begin with, then they go on from there. You know, they really thought they were kidding me, all this hospitality stuff and weren't they great to be sitting right there in a Negro's home, just like he was white! *That* kind of stuff. They're not fooling anybody. We'll just wait it out. Thank you, Mrs. Miller, Mr. Miller. You talked just great."

Paul's heart is quick. He embraced the man. He does that to a lot of people but it's not a stage trick. He means it. He said to the man, "I haven't got a sister."

"Me neither. You know what the Commies said to me? Paul Robeson for President, that's what they said. Now what the hell kind of a President would Paul Robeson make?"

"A President with the best baritone voice the White House ever had."

"And what good's a baritone voice going to be when he sits down with Khrushchev to argue?"

"Maybe they wouldn't argue."

The Negro laughed. "You've got something there, Mr. Miller. Thank you once more."

[221]

At one of our post-lecture seminars last winter, a man who I think was a little drunk or maybe just nasty stood up and said: "Mrs. Miller, it says in the program you're the most decorated woman in America. That right?"

"That's what I'm told. I didn't write the program."

"All right. Let's say you are. Now what exactly did you do? Spied on one chapter of one organization that might be a Communist front, might not, Government says it is. That what it all comes to?"

"That's it."

"You didn't blow up the Kremlin or free Hungary or turn up a master spy in this country, nothing like that? Didn't blow the whistle on Klaus Fuchs or discover Whittaker Chambers' pumpkins?"

"None of those."

"Didn't get beat up by any Commies or fed any of those truth drugs or kept in somebody's cellar till the Marines come and got you? Didn't help the CIA foil any saboteurs?"

"I'm afraid not."

"Then what's all the hollering for?"

The question was unanswerable. I have asked it of myself. I am grateful for the recognition granted me, but I have never hung a medal on myself or sought one. The man that night made me feel guilty for a while, a few times almost desolate.

Then along came the months of spring. One day we took the children to Disneyland, and the men who wore guards' uniforms were not guards but helpers, and everyone smiled and laughed without being ordered to. Some of the people there were rich and some poor and some in the middle, and not one to say that this was not as it should be. There were no marching bodies of men, no youth groups, no jaws locked tight with fervor beneath pale eyes fixed and glassy as they stared ahead to the glories of the motherland. This was a happy, wind-blown, casual lot, glorious in their disorganization, happy, even if they did not know it, in the assurance that in the hours to come, they could do whatever the spirit moved, wherever. Not once would there be a need to look backward over their shoulder while the stomach muscles knotted, the nerves pulled tight and the appetite suddenly quit cold.

Weeks later, in the political arena, there was a state primary. Three Presidential hopefuls got, each, thousands on thousands of popular votes. It was all pretty close as primaries go, and when it was done there was not a single political arrest. I doubt that more than a handful of persons in all the country stopped to think how wonderful that was. Even more wonderful is the fact that they didn't *have* to stop and think it.

I thought of it because I thought of the man who was let down by my not having blown up the Kremlin—a wanton and senseless act if ever I heard of one. By my not having been tortured, by my having failed to expose Klaus Fuchs. I looked at the news photos of the celebrants after the primary and read the final figures, and thought, I am a little part of this—I *am*.

Last spring, too, I was elected president of the Westwood chapter of B'nai B'rith. It had been months since I'd cried, but I cried then, the warmest, nicest kind of tears. It's strictly a local deal, but then, most things are. I was greatly honored but it was more than that. It was a group of my friends saying, "Come home again, Marion." Love given comes back. You just have to wait.

So it was a great occasion and we went to Disneyland again. "*Again!*" Bobby, six, says, "*Again!*" as though everything were surfeit. He is a solemn child and too young yet to say anything

[223]

cute for cuteness' sake. He slept in my lap going home and woke up when we were in the driveway. Still more asleep than awake, he said:

"That makes twice. I hope when I grow up I can go to Disneyland whenever I want to."

Into his hair, I said: "I hope so, too, Bobby."

"What?"

"I said, I hope so, too, dear. Pick up your feet now, Mommy's got to get out of the car."

—THE END—